GIVE

ALSO BY MAGNUS MACFARLANE-BARROW

The Shed That Fed a Million Children:
The Mary's Meals Story

GIVE

*Charity and
the Art of Living
Generously*

Magnus MacFarlane-Barrow

WILLIAM
COLLINS

William Collins
An imprint of HarperCollins*Publishers*
1 London Bridge Street
London SE1 9GF

WilliamCollinsBooks.com

First published in Great Britain in 2020 by William Collins

1

Scripture quotations marked 'ESV' are from the ESV Bible (The Holy Bible, English Standard Version), copyright © 2001 by Crossway, a publishing ministry of Good News Publishers. Used by permission. All rights reserved.

Scripture quotations marked 'NJB' are taken from The New Jerusalem Bible, published and copyright © 1985 by Darton, Longman & Todd Ltd and Doubleday & Co., Inc., a division of Random House, Inc. and used by permission.

Magnus MacFarlane-Barrow asserts the moral right to be identified as the author of this work in accordance with the Copyright, Designs and Patents Act 1988

A catalogue record of this book is
available from the British Library

ISBN 978-0-00-836001-6

Typeset in Adobe Caslon Pro
Printed and bound in Great Britain by
CPI Group (UK) Ltd, Croydon

I dedicate this book to my parents.
Thank you for showing us that charity begins at home
but does not end there.

Contents

Introduction

Charity to me will always smell of freshly baked bread. During the summer of 1985, even as the man on the radio updated us on the Ethiopian famine and its mounting death toll, my mother was pulling yet another batch of loaves from our oven. She was supporting a local fundraising effort aimed at helping those facing imminent starvation. Each warm loaf was adding to the delicious aroma in our house, before being delivered to the village hall to be sold amid an assortment of donated home baking.

Beyond our village, across the whole country, a plethora of such fundraising events were taking place that summer, the world having been stirred into action by an extraordinary news report by BBC reporter Michael Buerk. From a refugee camp in Tigray, surrounded by the dead and dying, he had described to us 'the closest thing to hell on earth'. Among the many fundraising efforts born in response to that horror, one dwarfed all others in its scale and ambition.

On 13 July 1985, along with 30 per cent of my fellow human beings, I sat down to watch Live Aid on the television. For a teenager living in the pre-internet era, the opportunity to spend a whole day with my friends enjoying live performances by the superstars of rock and pop felt almost too good to be true.

It was a great day. We cheered the bands we were fans of and ridiculed the ones we didn't appreciate – although once or twice we had to begrudgingly admire even some of their performances. As the bands in Wembley played on into the evening, the US version began in Philadelphia and some live performances from there were also beamed back to us. No one said as much, as we joked and laughed and debated each artist's performance, but it felt as if we were part of something special. By now Bob Geldof was giving us regular reminders of what this spectacular event was all about – raising funds to help the 8 million people who faced starvation in Ethiopia. At one point in the evening, David Bowie, having belted out 'We Can Be Heroes, Just for One Day', introduced a short video. It was four minutes of the most harrowing images I had ever seen. Suddenly in the room with us were emaciated children with protruding ribs and bloated stomachs, the piercing scream of a child, a tiny bandaged corpse. It was deeply shocking. We took turns using the house phone to call and pledge our own donations. I think it might have been the first gift to charity I ever chose to make. (I had long been putting coins in the plate at Sunday Mass but that didn't feel very optional.) As I hung up the phone, having shared my bank card details and a very little of my summer job earnings, I was surprised by a fleeting, unfamiliar feeling; a stab of joy and a momentary yearning to be someone better – and for the world to be something better too. I don't think it was just the beer.

Aside from the trauma of watching Scotland play football in the World Cup, Live Aid is the only vivid recollection I have of watching something on television in my youth. I am not sure if the experience played any part in my later journey into overseas aid work – there were certainly other, more obvious, triggers that led me to that – but I do believe that event in the summer of 1985 had an influence on the way I, and others of my generation, feel about certain things. The advances in technology that enabled us to watch those simultaneous concerts and which brought us distressingly close to the suffering in Ethiopia were creating new neighbours in distant countries; both those who urgently needed our help and those with whom we could respond in solidarity. Live Aid not only made charity feel possible, it made it feel 'cool', to use a word of the time. Having grown up in a devout Christian family, I had a fairly well-developed understanding of, and belief in, our duty to help the poor. From earliest memory – long before our house became a bakery that summer – I had been witnessing acts of charity. Some, like the making of bread, were quite mundane while others, such as my parent's unlikely decision to foster a seven-year-old boy with serious health issues, were more radical. I was familiar too with the stories of saints of old and their heroic acts of charity, but even so, the message just felt a bit different when delivered by Neil Young or Elvis Costello and received in the company of my best friends. For better or worse, without us knowing it, the era of celebrity-led charity campaigning had just been born.

Seven years after enjoying Live Aid, my brother and I watched another harrowing report on the television, this time about refugees whose lives had been devastated by the war that was tearing apart the former Yugoslavia. Our response on this occasion was very different. We made a little appeal to friends and family for donations of basic supplies and, having been given them in astonishing quantities, we took one week's holiday from our jobs (we were salmon farmers) to drive the gifts from Scotland to a refugee camp near Medjugorje in Bosnia–Herzegovina. I had no notion then that this would lead to the founding of a new charity which would eventually become Mary's Meals – a global movement which, today, sets up community-owned school feeding programmes in the world's poorest nations, providing over 1.6 million children with a daily meal in a place of education.

Like the founders of Live Aid, I had no relevant qualifications to lead this work, having simply been moved to act (in a much less ambitious way) by compassion for the suffering people brought close to me by the media. Nor did I have any long-term plan. The journey I set out on twenty-eight years ago has become my life's work only because that initial outpouring of kindness to our first appeal has never let up. That first trickle of donations has grown into a mighty river fed by little acts of love performed by hundreds of thousands of people all over the world in support of our mission. In Malawi alone, where over 30 per cent of the primary school population eat Mary's Meals each day, over 85,000 impoverished volunteers freely offer their time to cook and serve the hungry children of their communities. Meanwhile, in many wealthier countries, a vast army of volunteers, young and old, organise fundraising events, give public talks and take part in sponsored activities in order to provide the funds required to buy the ingredients for each meal. Each day we receive donations of all sizes made by those willing to share what they have so that others might at least eat. Children in primary schools collect coins and sell homemade baking, while their parents might commit monthly donations from their bank accounts. And while most of our support consists of these humble, unheralded deeds of charity, sometimes gifts of spectacular size, or representing radical life choices, are also presented amid this assortment of startling goodness. And each year as the number and value of these gifts grow, so does the number of children being fed.

The story of Mary's Meals suggests that charity is alive and well. And in many ways, indeed it is. However, this is only one story. There have been many less happy ones pertaining to charity during the same span of time. Charities seem to provoke consistent criticism, and a few have even been the cause of great scandal. Several concerns about how charities do things never seem to go away entirely: 'Charity CEOs are paid far too much!' or 'They just waste our donations on high overheads!' are among the familiar refrains.

In 2015, Olive Cooke, a ninety-two-year-old English charity volunteer, took her own life after being hounded by charity begging letters. Three years later, the high-profile sex abuse scandal initially relating to Oxfam staff in Haiti dominated headlines around the world, deepening further a crisis in public confidence. A survey that year, carried out by the Charities Aid Foundation in the UK, found that only 50 per cent of people 'agreed that charities were trustworthy', while a similar survey in the USA revealed that less than one in five Americans 'highly trust' charities. On taking up her post as the Chair of the Charity Commission for England and Wales in 2018, Baroness Stowell declared that their extensive independent research showed that 'people now trust charities no more than they trust the average stranger they meet on the street'.

Charity, in some quarters, has a bad name, her reputation tarnished by behaviour not fit to be associated with her. And each fresh scandal provides a new opportunity to ask other more fundamental questions. 'Does aid do more harm than good?' is one I first heard asked in the aftermath of Live Aid. Accusations that some of the funds raised had been siphoned off by the Ethiopian government, whose policies had played a huge part in causing the famine in the first place, led to suggestions that Bob Geldof's intervention had actually exacerbated the problem. As the years went by people pointed out that Ethiopia remained as poor as ever despite all the support given, and queried whether charitable efforts such as Live Aid just mask the underlying causes of poverty rather than helping address them.

Perhaps we were being simplistic and naïve that summer of 1985, carried away by a heady aroma of baking bread and rock-star righteous anger. Are those who persist in donating to charities just incurably gullible? And is the very concept of charity itself out of date – supplanted by things more sophisticated? For those of us who want to make the world better, maybe it is time to move on and engage in efforts aimed at supporting growth in the economy, international human development, the environment and political change?

There is no doubt that some aspects of Live Aid were flawed. The fact that no African artist graced the stages of Wembley or the JFK Stadium is cringe-inducing. The dramatic upturn in the careers of many Live Aid performers and their subsequent financial success is also, perhaps, troubling. And it is probably reasonable to suggest that the relationship with the government of Ethiopia could have been handled differently.

However, Live Aid and our response to it clearly did change things. It eventually prompted the international community to release enough surplus food stocks to end the famine. One million people died unnecessarily, but a much higher percentage of the 8 million people who faced starvation at one point might otherwise have succumbed. And surely Live Aid played a part in the subsequent change in attitude towards international aid by Western governments and helped inspire some of the effective campaigns that have targeted debt relief and fairer trade arrangements in the years since? After all, amid the multitudes who tuned in to watch the event, in addition to aspiring salmon farmers were future prime ministers and presidents. And the fact that in the years since, more timely, robust international responses have meant that no famine has ever resulted in a death toll like that seen in Ethiopia is another testament to the positive changes induced by that effort.

The debate about the merits and flaws of Live Aid corresponds to a broader one about charity and aid in general. One of the obstacles to productive discussion on these topics is a confusion about the scope and purpose of certain interventions. For example, Band Aid (the organisation founded to organise Live Aid and other related initiatives) never set out to lift Ethiopia out of poverty, and yet it was criticised for not doing so. Even the name itself should have pointed to the fact that this was always about relieving the immediate suffering caused by a human catastrophe. The objective was to save lives, not to tackle the underlying causes of hunger. The emaciated people of northern Ethiopia, days from death, were not in a position to await the outcome of some long-term development plan.

A better shared understanding of, and genuine respect for, different types of charity is much needed. However, while more clarity on this is an essential starting point, it will not alone restore faith in charity. For the *way* in which we carry out our work of charity is as important as the end results. Even if an organisation has developed a laser-sharp focus and the most efficient systems, but along the way has lost respect for those it serves, it will sooner or later become a scandalous thing. A charity that has established incredibly sophisticated fundraising techniques but has somehow forgotten that the people whose support they seek are humans who love, not ATM machines that just spit out money, is no longer worthy of the name. And even if they are implementing the most robust financial systems, when charities no longer revere each gift entrusted to their care as precious and unique, no matter their size, they are heading for a fall.

Charity is love. When we forget that, we horribly diminish this most noble human virtue. To be tasked with organising charity is no small responsibility. When we do it well, we elevate charity and help people to understand more about the wonder of humanity and the wonder of themselves. We can help both the giver and receiver of charity to become more fully human and to have more meaningful, more joyful lives. We can create places for faith, hope and love to flourish and thus allow the impact of our efforts to ripple out from the specific cause we are addressing to help create even more fundamental change in the world – change that can be subtle and substantial at the same time. But when we fail in our stewardship of charity, we can crush the human spirit and provide new reasons for cynicism, selfishness and even despair. We can encourage people to turn inwards instead of outwards. We cause harm that also ripples out beyond our particular failure – further damaging a broken world.

For many years my co-workers and I have been grappling with questions about the essence of charity and how to be its good stewards. In the face of our own mistakes and doubts, we have repeatedly been challenged and lifted up by those carrying out their little acts of love in support of our particular mission. They have spurred us on to try again and again to get it right; to renew our efforts to live up to the standards of charity that they, our supporters, set; to attempt to return always to a belief that those of us who are lucky enough to be employed in this work are servants of love – a love received and given.

And so we keep asking questions of ourselves. How do we best exercise stewardship of the resources entrusted us? How do we maintain a deep, authentic respect for those we serve and those who support our work? How do we define our mission in regard to where our responsibilities begin and end? How do we build appropriate relationships with governments and other key stakeholders? Are the values and approaches that served us well when we were a very small organisation still relevant to us today when millions of people in many different countries have a stake in our mission? I believe that only through finding answers to these questions and trying to put them into practice on a daily basis can we become stewards more worthy of the task of organising charity.

But journeys into charity are not only important for those of us involved in running charitable organisations – they are vital for anyone who wishes to become a better person. How we practise charity defines us as individuals. The way we encourage and foster it will shape the future of our societies. And yet, today more than ever, despite charity becoming a conspicuous part of Western culture, it is questioned, misunderstood and sometimes ridiculed. It might even be said that charity is currently suffering an identity crisis. But our fractured world, in which the loudest voices are so often egotistical, would do well to listen to the quiet voice of charity; to learn from it and to celebrate it – even if authentic charity does not seek that for itself.

And by practising charity more fully we will come to know ourselves more fully. We might discover along the way that it is not only the poor person over there that needs charity, but ourselves too. Within our very selves we may even discover famines – parts of us starved of love – or areas of darkness into which we have never before ventured. These journeys into charity might take us beyond the monthly direct debit donation we rarely think about (good though that is), or the sponsored run with our friends that is mainly fun (good though that is) and ask us to embrace things that involve risk and discomfort. Our relationship with charity can be a key that opens previously locked rooms where our greatest treasures lie in wait – where gems such as joy, peace and a deeper sense of meaning and purpose glint and glimmer in the dark.

But these journeys can be difficult. Maps are hard to come by and treacherous terrain can prompt us to turn back towards the comfort of home. And this would be a tragedy – especially because the joy to be found by those who persevere is one that can transform our lives. The happiest people I have ever met are the most charitable people I have ever met. And they are the people who will surely also have the biggest impact on the world in which we live – and its future – even if that might not always be immediately apparent. Things I have seen on my own journey thus far leave me in no doubt that even good deeds that seem very tiny to us can reverberate across oceans and even down through generations, causing all sorts of joy that would not otherwise be felt, in the lives of people who might seem very far removed from us.

During those first days of trying to help the people of Bosnia I fell in love with charity. I became enthralled by it. I was fascinated by those I saw practising it in ways that made me want to become a better person. I have been on that journey ever since and the truth is that sometimes I wonder if I have travelled any closer to my destination. Despite all these years enrolled in this very privileged school of charity, I am still a novice when it comes to practising it. Some seem to find this much easier than others and, in this matter, I have not been blessed with much talent. But I persist in the knowledge that God loves a trier and that charity is something within reach of each one of us at every moment – not just those with certain attractive personalities, or those who have chosen certain vocations or professions, or those with a particular education or adherence to a certain creed.

The work of Mary's Meals, which has spread around the world in a way I could never have planned or even imagined, has been fuelled by charity – by lots of little acts of love. By witnessing such acts countless times, I feel like I have come to know what real charity looks like, even though it might manifest itself in very different ways across diverse cultures and situations. The poor, the rich, rock stars, children, the elderly – all of us – are capable of the most beautiful and startling acts of charity that can change us and the world around us for the better.

I dare to write this book about charity then, not because I am a star pupil or an expert practitioner, but because this protracted journey of mine has allowed me to befriend many who are. While visiting distant famines or local school assemblies, in the aftermath of earthquakes and challenging sermons, and in the face of child hunger and adult surplus, I have encountered radical acts of charity being performed by profoundly charitable people. Their acts of love have surprised and challenged me. They have made me ask questions and they have renewed my desire to understand better what charity is. Through them, I have also come to believe, that where we see authentic charity, we see God.

When I hear charity misrepresented or belittled, I feel almost as if someone has spoken that way about my own mother, even as she quietly goes about the business of kneading another lump of dough in her desire to share some of the bread that belongs to all. For charity is too precious a gift to be disparaged and demeaned without defence. She is too crucial in our personal quest to become more fully human to be distorted by ill-chosen words and lazy rhetoric. And she is too wonderfully distinct to be confused with something she is not, and certainly too noble to allow wickedness to cower beneath the shelter of her name.

And that is why, despite not knowing all the answers, I have chosen to write this book.

1

'We Have It in Our Hearts'

The whole earth is the tomb of heroic men and their
story is not only given on stone over their clay but
abides everywhere without visible symbol woven
into the stuff of other men's lives.

PERICLES

Acts of charity let light into the world. This is more obvious
when they take place in the dark.

On 12 January 2010, less than an hour after a devastating
earthquake hit the Haitian capital of Port-au-Prince, night
fell. Even before the sun had set beneath the Caribbean hori-
zon, many were already in darkness, trapped and crushed
beneath piles of broken concrete and twisted metal. Many
died instantly, followed by thousands more during the ensuing
days and weeks. Of a total population of 3 million people,
around 220,000 lost their lives, another 300,000 people were
injured and over 1.5 million were left homeless. The term
'humanitarian disaster' is, perhaps, overused but on this occasion it felt like an understatement.

The tremors that devastated Port-au-Prince, which climbs from the dockside area up steep, eroded mountainsides, lasted only 35 seconds. Given that no one had experienced a significant earthquake in Haiti in living memory, very few would have realised what was occurring in those moments, during which ceilings began to fall on their heads and the ground heaved beneath their feet. Even after the strange deep thundering noise had stopped and been replaced by screams and pleading prayer, no clear sense of what had just occurred could have been possible. Certainly no one, from their own limited vantage point, could have had any notion of the scale of it. It would have been catastrophic and life-changing for each individual even if this event had just engulfed their own street or school or hospital, never mind the reality that a large city had just been devastated by this nameless thing.

One scientist later estimated that the force unleashed that afternoon on Port-au-Prince and the surrounding areas was the equivalent of thirty-five Hiroshima bombs. However, this disaster didn't fall from the sky, but emanated from an event 6 miles below the town of Leogane, 16 miles west of the city. The rubbing of two tectonic plates, which had been moving innocuously past each other for a few millimetres each day for many years before the earthquake, and which will probably continue to do so for many years to come, released the energy that so violently shook the relatively soft and crumbly ground to which the city clung.

It is not so easy to be precise about where an act of charity originates in a person. I think most of us would say it begins in the heart; a feeling of compassion which normally precedes any reasoned decision to act. We know that often the journey from our heart to our head (and back again, sometimes) can be a long and complex one. That night in Port-au-Prince the survivors did not have the luxury of having much time to think much about what to do. Amid the agony and mayhem people began to act: fathers and mothers responding to their family's screams beneath the rubble by digging with their bare hands; bloodstained school children carrying friends who couldn't walk towards hospitals that no longer existed; a small mother carrying a large broken son to who knows where; everyone all the while covered in a coat of white dust. Around some piles of immovable, contorted concrete slabs people huddled to speak words of comfort to dying loved ones below. Strangers helped wounded strangers, aiding and carrying each other in an exodus towards empty spaces – like a whole throng of Simons of Cyrene.

In the days and weeks after the earthquake, an enormous global outpouring of help and goodness was directed towards Haiti. Thousands rushed to donate to various appeals. A wide assortment of people and organisations from all over the world were drawn to Port-au-Prince in order to try to help – myself among them. While many of those co-ordinated efforts of people from outside Haiti should be lauded (and have been quite often), they should surely seem small when compared to the innumerable heroic acts of charity – most of them forever unrecorded – carried out by the Haitian people themselves in response to this previously unimaginable horror. That local response, though, should probably have been expected. It should be no surprise that an irrepressible people whose forefathers and mothers gloriously defeated Napoleon and slavery, and who have battled tirelessly with every kind of cruel injustice through many generations since, would respond to this latest calamity with such strength and with such love for each other. And perhaps any group of people, even one that hadn't experienced a history like that of Haiti, would respond heroically to such suffering among their own families and communities, discovering depths of love and strength which had previously gone untapped. We know that human beings are like that, and yet each time such acts prompt in us new feelings of wonder and awe. When a darkness covers the earth, very quickly little lights begin to flicker among the ruins, as they did that unforgettable night in Port-au-Prince, attracting around them close knots of people who can hold each other and wait for dawn.

I wish that the heroism of the Haitian people in the aftermath of the earthquake had been better reported. It would have been good for the world to have learnt more about that rather than hearing messages which reinforced stereotypical generalisations about endemic corruption and lawlessness. Those things do exist in Haiti, and are significant challenges that should be reported on, but not in an exaggerated, lazy way. There are serious consequences to such journalism and political rhetoric. When we portray a country like Haiti in this manner, we suggest it is completely reliant on outsiders to come and solve the problems it faces. Some reporting after the earthquake gave the impression that only foreign aid workers were pulling people from the rubble and that the aid efforts' biggest challenges were the lawlessness and inefficiency of the country. It is true that some areas of Haiti suffer high levels of violence, and that the capacity of the government and key national institutions is very limited. These realities made it a very difficult place to work effectively long before the earth-quake. However, creating an impression that Haiti was at best passively waiting for aid, or at worst actively undermining or obstructing it, would be to tell a terrible lie about that multitude of dust-covered, bloodstained individuals carrying out extraordinary acts of goodness.

Indeed, it would be to slander humanity more generally to suggest that people would wait passively for outside help to arrive rather than engage in spontaneous acts of individual kindness, like those who poured out kindness in the flickering light of candles after that cruel earthquake. While it is certainly necessary, in the face of great human suffering, to move beyond that chaotic phase towards something more organised and cohesive, among those instinctive actions we can sometimes witness the most pure and inspiring examples of charity. And to see the splendour of a truly selfless act is to be reminded of how astonishing and wonderful human beings are. Those glimpses can leave us with a desire to become more fully human ourselves: they can move us from looking inwards to looking outwards; they can transform our world into a place full of hope and possibility. They can leave us, too, with a desire to understand better what it is that inspires people to do these things.

Once, in Malawi, we decided to conduct a survey in an effort to shed light on that very question. We conducted a whole series of meetings in communities across Malawi where tens of thousands of volunteers – without any financial reward – give their time to cook meals each day for the children attending their local school. They are part of a vast army of porridge cooks spread across every district of the country, from Karonga in the north to Nsanje in the south.

We arrived at one village school, perched in the lee of a steep, rocky mountainside, long before the children, but the volunteers had been there for some hours already. As we climbed out of our car, we could see their fires glowing under enormous pots of porridge which some ladies were stirring with huge paddles that looked like oars. They were expecting our arrival and left their simmering porridge to sit with us in the dusty sparse grass of the empty playground. One unwrapped a baby from the cloth that had held him safely on her back and began to feed him.

We wanted to better understand their motives, to avoid the risk of taking them for granted and to ensure we found the right ways to recruit others like them in new villages as our work expanded. What was it that led these woman (and a much smaller number of men) to give up their time in order to cook and serve the free school meals for the children of their communities? What compelled them to arrive here each morning, long before dawn, to light those fires? Why take on that extra responsibility, knowing that the remainder of the day was going to be taken up with the exhausting work of survival? They would be planting, digging, weeding, pounding, carrying and chopping their way through another day, often while hungry and sick, in one of the ten poorest nations on Earth.

As most of the women who sat with us had never had the chance to go to school themselves – unlike the children they were volunteering to cook for – we conducted the surveys in the form of group discussions based on a standard list of questions. During the conversation on this particular morning, as the dawn began to brighten and warm, we posed our core question once again: 'Why do you do this?' A thin woman, with a shy smile cleared her throat.

'Because we have it in our hearts,' she said quietly, her smile growing like the huge rising sun behind her.

Charity is probably the best word to describe the thing in that woman's heart. Charity is an Old English word originally meaning 'Christian love of one's fellows' or 'benevolence for the poor'. It is derived from the Latin word *caritas*, which in turn is a translation of *agape*, the Greek word for a particular type of love; God's love for man and man's love in turn for God, including that expressed through his love of neighbour.

The earliest English translations of the Bible used the word 'charity' when translating *caritas* or *agape*, but later versions have tended instead to use the word 'love'. While it is a wonderful word, 'love' has a multitude of meanings – meanings that have their own separate words in many other languages. So when translated into English, the same word that St Paul uses in his famous letter to the Corinthians ('Love is patient, love is kind ...') is also sung in a thousand pop songs about romance, is spoken by a mother to her child and is used to express a desire for a drink on a hot day (in my case, usually in the form of 'I would *love* a beer.'). It is correct to say that charity means love – but only if we mean a particular kind of love.

And the use of the word 'charity' today can cause similar confusion. It covers not only that particular type of Christian love but more generally, any activity related to helping those in need, whether it be those of an individual or the organised initiatives that enable groups of people to help other groups of people – sometimes in faraway places. In addition, 'charity' can refer to efforts aimed at meeting immediate basic needs, tackling injustice, addressing the underlying causes of suffering or aiding longer-term human development. Charity today also includes helping animals and the planet more generally, although such activities can indirectly improve the lives of people too. To add to the potential confusion, in addition to being the name of a virtue or the activity prompted by it, 'charity' can also mean an organisation or body responsible for carrying out such work. It is certainly a hard-working word capable of some impressive multitasking.

Charity, in most of those senses, seems to have existed long before Christians began using the word. Perhaps charity is as old as humanity itself. The philosophies of the Ancient Greeks and Chinese incorporated some philanthropic ideas, while certain aspects of the belief systems of Native Americans and the civilisations of sub-Saharan Africans pointed towards ideas of sharing with those in need long before the colonialists arrived. And certainly beliefs and practices closely related to charity are central tenets of every major world religion.

In Hinduism, Buddhism and Jainism, the practice of charity is called *daana*. In sacred texts, *daana* has been described as 'any action of relinquishing the ownership of what one considered or identified as one's own and investing the same in a recipient without expecting anything in return'. *Daana* encourages the cultivation of generosity and an attitude of detachment, and can take the form of feeding or sharing directly with someone in distress or the support of philanthropic public initiatives aimed at empowering and helping many. The teaching and practice of *daana* is very ancient indeed and is first mentioned in a sacred text called the Rigveda, probably written between 1200 and 1500 BC.

I once witnessed a remarkable example of *daana* – a spontaneous outpouring of benevolence similar to the one which met the horror of that Haiti earthquake – in the immediate aftermath of the other colossal natural disaster to afflict humanity in the first ten years of this millennium, the Boxing Day Tsunami of 2004. Three days after that wave surged out of the Indian Ocean and killed a similar number of people to the Haiti earthquake (the victims on this occasion were spread across fourteen countries rather than one city), I watched local volunteers wearing homemade masks working through the wreckage of a coastal fishing village in Tamil Nadu, India. The overwhelming stench of death and the gut-wrenching screams of the bereaved made their job of recovering decomposing bodies even more hideous. Resolutely, hour after hour, and even after they had recovered 100 bodies from the mangled debris, they continued with the utmost dignity and gentleness, covering each corpse respectfully with a sheet before carrying it to the gaping hole on the beach. Some of the remains were of very small children, laid to rest while their parents cried in agony and held each other nearby. How could anyone find the strength to volunteer to do a job like that? They were driven that day not so much by their respect for the dead, but by their love of the living. The first step that had to be taken towards any kind of recovery and healing was this dreadful one, and so somewhere inside them they found the strength to move their feet and do this unavoidable thing.

And later that same day, in the nearby city of Chennai, hundreds of people not directly affected by the horror on the coast turned up at a relief centre bearing gifts of food, among them school children carrying mugs of rice – sharing what they had so that those who had lost everything could eat. It seems that every awful, distressing, human calamity can prompt an amazing, generous human response. And in this part of the world many call it Daana.

For the Jewish people *tzedakah* means 'righteousness', and its central place in the Torah, many centuries before Christ, laid the foundations on which Christian charity would later be built. It represents a religious obligation to behave in a way that is 'right and just'. Jews give *tzedakah* by helping the needy through donations of money, time or other resources. The Torah teaches that a tenth of your income should be given to 'righteous deeds or causes' (this practice of 'tithing' was later embraced by Christians). In the Middle Ages the influential Sephardic Jewish philosopher Maimonides listed eight levels of giving as written in the Mishneh Torah. The list, which has had a huge influence on Jewish charity ever since, extols things such as giving anonymously to a known recipient, giving before being asked and, at the top of the list, a very particular form of charity: 'giving an interest-free loan to a person in need; forming a partnership with a person in need; giving a grant to a person in need; finding a job for a person in need, so long as that loan, grant, partnership, or job results in the person no longer living by relying upon others'.

When I first read this centuries-old decree, it made me think of a story I had just heard from a close friend. His brother, having some years earlier emigrated to the USA, had recently fallen on hard times. Having plummeted through a series of personal disasters related to drug and alcohol addictions, he had ended up homeless on the streets of New York. His desperate poverty and psychological state left my friend back home in Scotland fearing greatly for his brother's life. My friend and his family had tried to help in various ways but to no avail – his brother had reached a point of self-imposed isolation that made it impossible for his family to reach him.

One day, as my friend's brother sat on a park bench in Central Park, watching the tourists walk by, an elderly lady sat down beside him. After a little while she looked at him and asked him how he had come to be living like this and he began to tell her a little of his story. She invited him to meet her there again, and on their next meeting he poured out his life to the stranger. On their third meeting the little Jewish mother explained that she had had a son of similar age to him who died. She offered him her spare room rent free, with a set of firm rules including total abstinence from drugs and alcohol, until he got his life back on the rails. He accepted the startling offer and when I last heard he was rebuilding a new, better life. Through the 'partnership' this elderly lady chose to form with a homeless stranger, she has enabled him to journey towards becoming a 'person no longer living by relying on others'. I have no idea how deliberate it was on her part, but she was certainly practising *tzedakah* in a wonderful way.

In some respects *zakat*, one of the 'five pillars' on which Islam is based, is similar to *Tzedakah* – in fact, some scholars believe the word *zakat* derives from *tzedakah*. *Zakat* also obliges Muslims to give a prescribed amount to good causes – an amount usually set as 2.5 per cent of savings over a certain minimum threshold – and in some Islamic countries this is obligatory in law and collected as a tax. In addition to *Zakat*, Muslims may also practise *sadaqa*, that is, voluntary charity, which as well as donating to those in need can even include smiling at people.

Some Muslim doctors who I met one dark frightening night in Somalia were doing more than smiling at people. It was during the terrible famine of 2011. They were from South Africa and were there to volunteer their urgently needed expertise in a health clinic. I was there with a load of food we had flown in from Malawi. We had landed there at a particularly messy moment in a war which had, by then, already inflicted twenty-one years of suffering. At that point Mogadishu was said to be the most dangerous city in the world; it was teeming with men in ragtag uniforms with AK-47s slung over their shoulders and there was uncertainty as to which neighbourhoods were controlled by which faction. My nerves had not been helped on our first evening there when, as we were being shown to our shared sleeping quarters by our host – a teenage Somali man with perfect, gently spoken English – there was a huge explosion close by. It made me jump. Our young host turned to me.

'Don't worry. Don't worry,' he said, as if soothing a very young child.

'It was just a bomb.'

The doctors and I laughed a lot about this over our late evening meal together, but the next morning our mirth died when we began to encounter those we had come to try to help. Hundreds of thousands of people had recently arrived in the capital in a desperate search for food. We began hearing the stories of women who had walked over 150 kilometres – some of them had seen their children die on the way. Others were caring for children not their own, the children's parents having died in a famine that had already taken the lives of tens of thousands.

Fartune was one of the mothers who told us her desperate story as she stood in a long queue for food holding her sick child, Pinte. His head looked grotesquely large compared to his tiny body and his swollen eyes could no longer see. He was three years old and had been sick for six weeks. Until now Fartune had never had the chance to take Pinte to a doctor or receive any medical help for her child. She told us she had another three children at 'home' (a hastily erected hut made of sticks and plastic, surrounded by thousands of other similar temporary abodes). We asked her how those other children at home were.

'Yes, they are fine,' she said, before adding. 'Apart from the malnutrition. We never have enough to eat.'

I didn't get much more time to talk with the doctors during those days, absorbed as we were in our respective missions to feed and treat so many sick people. But late at night, back at our base, our conversation turned to matters of faith, as is the case sometimes when in extreme situations. We talked about our different religious beliefs and about why our young people seemed to be losing their faith; about secularism, materialism, social media, the need for fellowship and community. We talked about how our faith, if it is sincere, must impel us to do works of charity. We talked too about our devotion to a Jewish woman, Mary the Mother of Jesus (who they call Miriam) – mother of the Christ, mother of the Prophet. They loved the fact I worked for an organisation who held her as their patron. Once again it seemed to me that in each of our hearts something similar had been etched despite our very disparate backgrounds and beliefs. And each morning, as my friends assembled outside on their prayer mats for their morning devotion, I said my rosary and pondered some things in a new way, grateful for fresh perspectives.

Even louder than the call to prayer, echoing across the war-weary city, and the thunderous blast that had made my heart leap on the night of our arrival, the clarion call of charity had summoned each of us here from our different corners of the Earth. It is a very beautiful thing when *sadaqa* or charity or *tzedakah* or *daana* – or whatever we wish to call that thing we have in our hearts – brings us together like that, in the service of strangers. I watched a particularly dramatic example of this on one occasion while visiting a little Mary's Meals project in a slum near New Delhi.

There I met Angela, a high-caste Hindu, who was volunteering her time to teach a group of *dalit* children. For the largest part of each day, these children search in rubbish heaps for things they can sell to help support their families. There were about ninety of them gathered around Angela's little blackboard, on which were written letters of the Hindi alphabet that they were taking turns to name. They had been drawn from their all-consuming work by the daily meals that were being cooked in the adjacent courtyard and by Angela's smile, which seemed to illuminate the gloomy little room in which they sat. The room itself was a gift. A Muslim gentleman, whose little house it was part of, was the free giver of that gift, allowing the raggedy group to make it their classroom for a short time each day while his adjoining courtyard became their kitchen and dining room. Meanwhile the delivery of the food and its cooking was being overseen by the project's administrator, a stubby nun adorned in the black habit of her order.

Did you hear about the Muslim, the Hindu and the Catholic? That has to be the opening line of a great joke – and maybe it is – but it is also a question I like to answer by telling the story of that little trinity of goodness, meeting in a country deeply wounded by sectarian hatred, where the caste system condemns millions to spend their childhood working instead of learning. The need of those dishevelled little ones – so often an object of scorn and derision – was drawing together representatives of three world religions.

What is striking, from even a cursory glance at the place of 'charity' across very different cultures and religions, are the very strong common threads. The idea that charity improves life for the giver, on Earth and beyond, as well as for the receiver, is one that seems to transcend creeds. That everything we have is a gift from God to be shared is another. There are also key differences, however, that become even more obvious as we explore further the practice of charity – especially the distinct nature of Christian charity, which smashes the boundaries and obligations of giving by proclaiming every person in need as deserving of our charity, not just those sharing our faith or ethnic group or political view, but in fact even our enemies.

The story Jesus told of the Good Samaritan is among the most famous of His parables. He told it when a lawyer asked Him how to inherit eternal life. Jesus initially replied with a simple confirmation of the ancient teaching of the Old Testament: 'You shall love the Lord your God with all your heart and with all your soul and with all your strength and with all your mind, and your neighbour as yourself.' (Luke 10:26–28, ESV)

It was only when the lawyer then enquired who his neighbour was that Jesus answered with a story that has resonated through the ages, helping to shape Christian, and other, works of charity ever since. His tale was the one of the 'Good Samaritan' who had stopped to help a man lying badly injured after being attacked by robbers. Two others – a priest and a Levite – had passed the man without helping. But this Samaritan (and Jesus clearly did not accidentally make the hero of His story a Samaritan – Samaritans were foreigners, despised and considered heretics by the Jews) showed what it was to love your neighbour. And, crucially, he also revealed who our neighbour is – every human being in need of our help. As Dorothy Day, a radical modern-day disciple of Jesus, put it two thousand years later, 'The Gospel takes away our right for ever to discriminate between the deserving and the undeserving poor.'

But, of course, charitable activities are not only practised by those of faith. Even as the Western world has become rapidly more secular it has retained and developed a strong brand of humanitarianism – a type of charity that has clearly been informed by its Judeo-Christian heritage, even while, ironically, that heritage is being rejected and forgotten. This modern form of secular charity is vast in its scale and spectacular in its practice. It holds a very prominent place in society. Politicians, pop stars, entrepreneurs – in fact celebrities and influential people of all sorts – are the enthusiastic leaders and ambassadors of this ubiquitous charity of the modern age, which is presented in TV extravaganzas, star-studded events, high-street shops, cause-related marketing campaigns, sponsored events in our schools, 5-kilometre runs in our parks and even by filming ourselves having buckets of ice-cold water poured over our heads. Supporting charities has become an extremely popular mass-participation pastime.

But while certain cultures and belief systems have encouraged and celebrated charity, others sometimes do the opposite. For example, the impact of Communism's antagonism towards charitable activities, viewing them as an encroachment on the role of government and a legacy of religion (the 'opium of the people', as Karl Marx referred to it) can be seen even today in Communist and post-Communist states. A global survey on participation in charitable activities revealed that in 2017 only 14 per cent of the people of China donated money to a charity, placing it third from bottom on the global league table. In comparison, in Indonesia, at the top of the table, 78 per cent of people gave donations. The same exercise found that while in 2017 only 11 per cent of those living in the Russian Federation volunteered their time for an organisation, 47 per cent of Liberians did so, despite inhabiting one of the poorest nations on the planet.

In fact, curiously, it sometimes seems that the poor give more (as a proportion of what they have) than the rich. In the early days of our own mission this was something we experienced in quite a dramatic way. Each week we would make appeals for food in supermarkets, inviting shoppers to place donations of dried and tinned foods in our trolley for us to load into our van and drive to the hungry refugees in Bosnia–Herzegovina. The response to each of those appeals was incredibly generous but especially so in the more deprived parts of town. This became quite a marked pattern over a number of years.

So, while the charity that resides in the human heart might be universal, it is clear that our circumstances, cultures, religions and ideologies have an enormous influence on whether these feelings of compassion are acted upon, and if so, in what way.

But regardless of our environment, the charity we feel in our heart remains an intrinsic part of our humanity. This love for the other, even the stranger, seems to dwell in us – and doesn't need to wait for some disaster or cataclysmic event. It is acted out quietly every day, in modest ways and in all sorts of places.

One dark night I was queuing for a train ticket outside an obscure railway station in Bihar, Northern India. There were rows of people sleeping on the pavement around the main entrance, huddled under blankets. As I waited to be served, I noticed an elderly lady sitting up with her blanket around her. She coughed an agonised, rasping cough that made me shudder. After a few moments she climbed slowly and very unsteadily to her feet. She glanced down and noticed that a baby beside its sleeping mother was uncovered and she bent down, with some difficulty, to very carefully tuck him in before walking off to spit out what her coughing had brought up.

On another occasion, in Uganda's capital, Kampala, I visited St James' Primary School. In the playground Beatrice was sitting in the baking dust. She was nine years old. It was

1.30 pm and she was devouring her school meal – it was the first thing she had eaten that day and it was likely to be the last. She noticed that a distraught-looking classmate had no plate with him and had missed his serving. So she walked over to him and, without exchanging a word, they squatted beside each other in the dust and began to share the maize and beans from the plastic plate in front of them.

Ahead of structure and co-ordinated effort, with no need for recognition or thanks, and perhaps without knowing any theology, our hearts can sometimes no longer resist the impulse to act. Long before the journalist reports a misery, or an international appeal is launched, or planes carrying food arrive, charity is already burning in our hearts and igniting little fires in the gloom.

2

Charity in the Dock

> We must know ourselves well enough to recognise
> our own illusions ... enough to be able to tell when
> it is not the Charity of Christ that speaks in our
> hearts but only our own self pity ... or ambition, or
> cowardice, or thirst for domination.
>
> THOMAS MERTON

I landed in Port-au-Prince four days after the earthquake, just
as the response was making its transition from spontaneous
and chaotic (and no less heroic for it) to a more co-ordinated
and orderly phase. I had been propelled there by an unprecedented outpouring of goodness from our supporters all over
the world, and had come to assist in planning the next phase,
including agreeing immediate priorities and use of the funds
with which we had been entrusted. I walked from the runway
through a no-longer-functioning, half-collapsed terminal
building onto streets teeming with misery. A mob of children
begging for food beset us. It was early evening and in every
space between piles of concrete and twisted metal people were

looking for a place to sleep. I soon found myself doing something similar, although I had the luxury of Father Tom's courtyard.

Father Tom and his co-worker Doug are co-founders of an organisation called Hands Together, which we had been working with in Haiti for some years. They focus much of their work on the nearby, notorious slum of Cité Soleil, where hundreds of thousands live on what was a rubbish dump: they are Haiti's poorest of the poor, and endure a poverty as squalid, oppressive and violent as any I have witnessed.

I arrived at Father Tom's place during the short dusk of the tropics and, though I had stayed in this compound several times previously, I was finding it hard this time to get my bearings. The small pile of rubble that Father Tom and Doug pointed to as they recounted events surely could not be the remains of the substantial house that had accommodated volunteers and frequent visitors like me? I could see familiar twisted bits of green metal balcony railings and I thought of a moment during my first visit here four years earlier. It was early evening and I was sitting on the roof of the house with a co-worker from Scotland. We were praying together and trying to understand better what we had seen that day during our first visit to Cité Soleil. Father Tom had appeared up the little staircase to join us in prayer and had then spoken to us, trying to help us understand things there – the suffering, the history, the violence, the politics – while telling us several times that even after all these years he didn't understand it either. He disarmed us by telling us he wasn't even sure all his years' work here had really achieved anything.

And now I was looking at a pile of concrete and metal which had, until four days ago, been arranged in the shape of that house in which we had sat and prayed and made friends. Father Tom and Doug were doing their best to explain what had happened. It was distressing for them, but it seemed they needed to speak of it and I hoped that it was cathartic in some way. Two of the men who lived with them, and who had been in the house as it collapsed, had died. Doug and the other dazed survivors had dug with bare their hands, initially to try to save them, but in the end only to recover their bodies. We walked together a short way past the rubble to the back of the courtyard to pray where two simple wooden crosses marked their graves.

Meanwhile, their courtyard was becoming surprisingly well-ordered and a number of friends and co-workers were gathering to sleep there. An old bus parked in one corner was serving as accommodation for the women and children; in another some tin and tarpaulin had created a new temporary head office for Hands Together. I noticed that one of the high walls which had previously made this compound secure had toppled over. Under a tree Father Tom had created a little chapel. We all gathered there to pray together – our little, newly formed homeless community – before lying down on old mattresses recovered from the ruins to sleep. I stared at the stars above me and thought of childhood camping trips and my own children at home. Planes and helicopters were roaring incessantly across the sky. It was loud but reassuring. People and aid of all sorts were beginning to arrive. Later gun shots and shouts punctuated the night, together with screaming and groaning.

The next day was one of intense information-gathering and planning. What could we best do, as two small organisations working together, to relieve at least some of this enormous sea of suffering around us? We sat down that morning in the makeshift office to begin our discussions with Nelson, the Hands Together general manager who had lost his wife and children in the earthquake, and other local leaders of the Hands Together team. They personally were making the transition from instinctive, individual acts of charity towards something more co-ordinated and planned, while also just starting to deal with their own horrendous loss.

This step, from one to the other, occurs in the aftermath of any humanitarian disaster, when it becomes clear that the scale of suffering requires an organised reaction. It certainly doesn't mean that the personal, spontaneous kindnesses stop – God forbid that should ever happen – rather, it enables these to be co-ordinated and provides them with the tools they need to become more effective. This move towards co-ordinating and managing charity is also, in essence, what leads to the birth of new organisations. A desire to go beyond an initial informal act of goodness to create a new ongoing mission in order to meet an unmet need, which allows others to join and play their part, is what prompts the registration of a new organisation, the figuring out of objectives and the writing of a constitution. It is how Mary's Meals and a multitude of other charitable organisations were born.

Most studies of modern humanitarianism locate its origins in the eighteenth and nineteenth centuries. The Industrial Revolution gave rise to new types of human suffering; the plight of the new urban poor, the rights of women, the hunger of children and many other human sufferings prompted various political movements and charitable endeavours. This was also the era of Empire, fervent missionary activity and new kinds of internationalism. Taking advantage of their countries' empires, Christian missionaries took the gospel message to distant lands, but they also brought back a new awareness of life in the colonies and issues relating to human rights and poverty. This then became the era distinguished by the anti-slavery campaigns, which galvanised large numbers of people to fight together for the rights of people on another continent for the first time. And, when the abolitionists won their battle against slavery, new questions and needs arose in regard to support of the newly emancipated former slaves and their communities

Heroes emerged, such as Florence Nightingale, who became famous as 'The Lady with the Lamp' while caring for injured and sick soldiers during the Crimean War of the 1850s. She then set up the Nightingale Fund and began fundraising to set up a new Nightingale Training School for nurses in London. As well as being considered the founder of modern nursing, she was also a key figure in various campaigns for social reform, and among other things fought for the abolishment of unjust prostitution laws and for more effective hunger relief in India.

In 1863 the International Committee of the Red Cross (ICRC), often described as the first international humanitarian organisation, was founded by a Swiss businessman called Henry Dunant. Four years previously he had witnessed firsthand the battle of Solferino in northern Italy and the atrocious human suffering it caused. This led him to found an organisation with the purpose of providing humanitarian relief during times of war. Realising that in order to do this effectively the neutrality of the Red Cross would need to be recognised and respected by all parties in a war zone, he then instigated the ground-breaking work that led to the signing of the Geneva Convention.

It seems that the term 'humanitarianism' was first entering mainstream language at this time and the Red Cross led the way in attempting a definition of it. Their commentary on the Fundamental Principles of the Red Cross contains the following statement:

> Humanitarianism is a doctrine which aims at the happiness of the human species, or, if one prefers, it is the attitude of humanity towards mankind, on a basis of universality. Modern humanitarianism is an advanced and rational form of charity and justice. It is not only directed to fighting against the suffering of a given moment and of helping particular individuals, for it also has more positive aims, designed to attain the greatest possible measure of happiness for the greatest number of people. In addition, humanitarianism does not only act to cure but also to prevent suffering, to fight against evils, even over a long term of time. The Red Cross is a living example of this approach.

Part of the purpose of this new term, humanitarianism, was to make a distinction between this universal doctrine – something every person of good will could accept – and 'charity' as something understood to mean Christian love, or other doctrines inspired by religion. However we choose to define humanitarianism, war very often seems to inspire it. In the twentieth century the World Wars and their aftermaths compelled many new, charitable initiatives. Save the Children and Care International were born in response to the humanitarian crisis caused by the First World War, while Oxfam was founded during the Second. All three of those charities – like the ICRC before them and Médecins Sans Frontières (born during the Biafran War) since – have grown out of the horrors of war to become vast global charities today.

During the post-war period, as the European Empires began to disintegrate, it seemed that the aid and development efforts which had helped rehabilitate a broken Europe might be applied to the poverty and suffering now visible in the former colonies. After all, if the Marshall Plan, which saw the USA provide US$ 12 billion to Western Europe after the Second World War, could play a part (how big a part is debated by historians and economists to this day) in bringing about a remarkable recovery and record-breaking economic growth, and if organisations such as the Commission for Relief in Belgium, founded during the First World War by future US president Herbert Hoover, could save millions from starvation, then surely the world's poorest nations could be helped in the same way?

During the subsequent decades of the Cold War, and up to the present day, each major conflict or natural disaster has spawned new organisations. The lifespan of some of them lasts no longer than the crisis itself, while others take what they have learnt and the network of support they have formed and begin to apply these to future crises – or indeed ongoing projects in impoverished places. That is just how our work began.

When driving our first little consignment of donated aid from Scotland to Bosnia–Herzegovina in 1992, I remember us joining a ragtag convoy of vehicles, all on the same mission – the delivering of donated goods from various European countries to the refugee camps of the former Yugoslavia. Battered trucks, cars pulling trailers and converted camper vans, all bulging with precious gifts, were converging on the scene of that shockingly close Balkan war. Some flew their country's flag; others had painted or stuck the name of their mission on the side of their automobiles, naïvely hoping this might induce the border guards to show them mercy. I am sure some from the UN bodies and the large, established aid organisations must have laughed or shook their heads in horror as we passed – and I wouldn't blame them if they did – but there was something very uplifting about the spectacle too, rather like a latter-day mission to Dunkirk, when all those civilians sailed their little boats among the naval frigates, painfully aware of how small and inadequate they were in that unfamiliar and daunting setting, but doing it nonetheless.

Of those little missions to the former Yugoslavia, most completed their good deeds during those war years and then went back to their day jobs, but a few, like us, grew into something else. We certainly never originally intended that – we didn't envisage anything beyond just one local appeal for donated goods and one week's holiday from our jobs to drive a Land Rover full of aid to Bosnia–Herzegovina. And even when we first registered our organisation (then called Scottish International Relief), we didn't initially foresee that this might grow beyond the simple direct delivery of donated material aid from Scotland to Bosnia–Herzegovina. However, as we began to learn how to do things more effectively – both in terms of building support and in the delivery of aid to those in need – the idea of replicating it in order to help other suffering people, some of whom were now requesting us to do so, became a very convincing one – irresistible, in fact. And in this sense at least, the founding story of Mary's Meals is similar to that of many other organisations.

And so, with each passing decade and each new humanitarian disaster which stirs fresh charitable responses, the number of such organisations continues to grow. It is impossible to know for sure how many international humanitarian organisations there are today, but some estimate there are over 7,000 based in the West and working in other countries. These are known as international non-governmental organisations (NGOs), defined as being not dependent on government funding and with operations in at least two countries other than the one in which they are based. Even more striking, perhaps, is the scale to which some of them have grown. The very largest, such as World Vision, Care International or the ICRC, have annual incomes of over US$ 2 billion. A report on the sector in 2018 estimated that 570,000 people are now employed in international humanitarian charities globally, and that their total global budget is over US$ 27 billion – although it should be pointed out that around US$ 20 billion of that comes from governments. This is an important distinction because, even as far back as the Marshall Plan, 'government aid' was never so much an act of charity as a key strand of foreign policy.

At that point, as the new Cold War rivalry with the USSR kicked off, the security of their Western allies, and their influence over them, was crucial to the USA. The Marshall Plan supported those aims and, today, even a cursory glance at the biggest recipients of US and UK aid budgets reveals that current policies are not based on a simple charitable desire to help those who are most in need in the world. Neither Pakistan, which benefits most from UK funding, nor Israel, which has received nearly US\$ 3.2 billion from the USA, are among the poorest nations on Earth. In fact, Israel is ranked as a 'high-income country'. The objectives that drive political decisions on how to distribute this 'aid' are not some grubby secret. In 2018, Prime Minister Theresa May stated that 'Britain's aid budget would be used to promote British trade and political interests', while President Trump, during his first cabinet meeting of 2019, said: 'It's very unfair when we give money to Guatemala and to Honduras, and to El Salvador, and they do nothing for us.' Two months later the USA cut all its funding of humanitarian aid to all three countries.

However, while these leaders are not hiding their motives, it remains troubling that they call this kind of funding 'aid' and thereby create confusion among the public – and perhaps among humanitarian organisations too. As this is a journey into charity, rather than politics, I will not dwell on the political agendas at play, but this miscalling of an activity as 'aid' when it is very clearly something else is an important example of how certain things choose to present themselves as charity for their own ends and how damaging that can be. Certain criticisms and condemnations of charity can be misplaced because of this. And the charities that become dependent to a greater or lesser extent on this type of government funding are embracing another risk – the loss of clarity about their own focus and purpose.

This is just one of many complexities to be grappled with by charities working in international aid today. It is a very long way from a small homespun effort to provide direct help to some people suffering in a war that we saw reported on our televisions, to the management of organisations with tens of thousands of staff working in over a hundred countries, funded by myriad different sources and engaged in projects with a whole variety of objectives. The initial desire to help save the lives and relieve the suffering of some people will often lead to a desire to tackle the underlying cause of their problems. Then there will inevitably come the questions about justice, human development, economics, political change, advocacy, certain ideologies and now – more than ever before – the environment and its essential place in the better future of humanity.

We will encounter again some of these questions as we continue onwards on this exploration of charity, but what is already clear is that the bewildering diversity of activities which call themselves charity presents a huge challenge, as does the maintenance and organisational development of such gargantuan international bodies. How does a charity operating in scores of different countries, employing tens of thousands of staff, retain unity in adhering to its founding vision and values? When present in a multitude of environments and societies, how might it create and maintain its own distinct organisational culture? As the pressure grows to raise funds in order to grow, or just to meet existing obligations, how might fundraising efforts preserve a profound respect for their supporters or potential supporters? And when the organisation needs strengthening in order to deliver effectively, how might the required investments be made in a way that a public, who at times seem fixated on charities' 'overheads' or 'admin costs', can understand and support?

These are only a few of the plethora of thorny questions facing charities in the modern era. And in failing to satisfactorily answer some of them those of us leading charities have at times allowed their good names to be besmirched.

In recent decades a series of high-profile scandals relating to the running of charities have had an impact on how charities are perceived and the public's trust in them. These have included some very different types of alleged wrongdoing. Some have been cases of blatant fraud, such as that of William Aramony, who as President of the United Way had helped turn it into one of the USA's largest charities. He was convicted in 1995 of defrauding the organisation of US$ 1 million, which he used to fund lavish extra-marital affairs, among other things. Prior to being jailed for six years he had been lauded as a 'visionary' and a 'genius'.

Other damaging headlines have often related to the salaries of charity chief executives. Sometimes these salaries have been made public during the airing of some other scandal – for example, it was revealed that, when convicted, William Aramony had an annual compensation package of US$ 460,000.

In the UK there has been strong public feeling on this subject for many years, summed up nicely in this opening paragraph of an article published by the *Guardian* newspaper in January 2019: 'It says here in this letter you sent that £4 from me could help save a life. So how about your CEO takes £40,000 less salary next year and saves 10,000 lives?' This was a message received from a monthly donor by one of the UK's best-loved charities in August 2013, following sustained media coverage about the high pay of chief executives in the UK voluntary sector.

This recurring issue of salaries is often linked to 'administration costs' or 'high overheads' and sometimes to allegations of extravagant spending by charity bosses. The Wounded Warrior Project, one of the best-known organisations in the USA working with disabled and wounded veterans, hit the headlines for all the wrong reasons in 2016 when the media exposed its 'lavish spending'. It was reported that in 2014 alone, they spent US$ 26 million on conferences and meetings at luxury hotels – similar to the total amount they were spending on combat stress recovery. While other similar charities were contributing over 90 per cent of their funds to directly supporting veterans, The Wounded Warrior Project was spending only 60 per cent.

Meanwhile, in the UK, a high-profile London charity called Kids Company, a favourite of celebrities and politicians, many of whom seemed in thrall to its charismatic founder Camila Batmanghelidjh, spiralled into a financial meltdown and closed suddenly in August 2015. It left behind a string of empty promises and red faces within the government departments that had provided it with £46 million of public money despite repeated concerns that had been raised about how it was being run.

And then there was the very sad case of Olive Cooke, from Bristol, who took her own life at ninety-two years of age. She was the longest-serving poppy seller in the UK and supported numerous charities. It was revealed that by the time of her death she was receiving 180 letters from charities each month, and was also being plagued by their phone calls. Her family revealed that she had been suffering from depression, and they believed the pressure she felt she was being put under by the charities had contributed to her death. The fact that the charities she had chosen to support had been sharing her details with others provoked a public outcry. It prompted new interest in and criticism of aggressive fundraising techniques and led to reforms of charity fundraising regulation.

But the worst was yet to come. If the charity sector was already feeling a bit battered and bruised by this point, it was about to receive a much more devastating body blow.

Amid the debris of Port-au-Prince in the aftermath of the earthquake, we sat down for a meeting led by our Haitian co-workers, most of them victims themselves who had already been helping those around them in whatever way they could.

An early theme of that meeting was 'humility in action', a phrase that Father Tom and Doug used often and which resonated with our own approach at Mary's Meals. This phrase was to become a guide for our discussions and decision-making in those days. We needed to recognise from the outset that, in the face of a gigantic earthquake, we were very small and very insignificant. While we were committed to striving with all our strength to do whatever we could, and while we believed that we might, with God's help, ease the suffering of many, we also needed to be realistic about our own very obvious limitations as individuals and as a group. We needed to become clear about we should try to do and, perhaps even more importantly, what we should not try to do. Perhaps this sounds blatantly obvious, but not being properly grounded in this attitude – whether we are responding to an earthquake or a homeless person in front of us or making ongoing strategic decisions about our organisation – can be the root of all kinds of later problems.

It is this approach that eventually led the Mary's Meals mission to concentrate solely on one simple thing: the provision of one meal every day in a place of education. Each day, when serving those meals, we see other needs we would like to address, but we have chosen a focus that leads us back to doing one thing and trying to do it very well. And that requires a certain discipline, to resist the temptation that tells us we can do everything or that we have responsibility for everything. I am not suggesting every organisation should restrict itself to becoming specialists in only one simple activity: each organisation should have its own unique mission, identity and approach. I am only suggesting that a very common problem in this kind of work is the 'mission drift' that inevitably occurs if a certain kind of humility is not our starting point, and something we deliberately remind ourselves of on a regular basis. Of course, we can also go to the other extreme. A singular focus can be applied so sternly that we stifle all promptings of the heart, becoming cold even to the suffering person right in front of us as we tick our boxes and talk of targets reached. Or we can miss opportunities to learn or to innovate in ways that could help everyone move forward. These are real risks too, which I will return to, but on this hot January morning, surrounded by death, destruction and desperate need on an epic scale, it felt as if 'humility in action' was an essential starting point.

And then we began to gather information from the local co-workers in our midst, asking them for their thoughts on the most immediate needs. Most of them were from Cité Soleil and they explained to us that Cité Soleil was in some ways less dramatically affected than other parts of the city. The people there were certainly in urgent need of help, but ironically their resounding poverty had spared them in certain ways. When your home is constructed of salvaged rusty corrugated tin, it is much less likely to kill or maim you when shaken to the ground by an earthquake. The loss of life in Cité Soleil was relatively low as a result. Other basic human needs, which the people of Port-au-Prince now found themselves deprived of – electricity, water, healthcare – were things already lacking in Cité Soleil. There, every day had been a battle to survive even before the earthquake. Certainly, though, some needs had become more acute, and the insecurity in Cité Soleil meant few aid organisations would find it possible to operate. With Hands Together's huge experience of Cité Soleil and its deep connection with the community – in the form of relationships built over many years – it seemed obvious that this was where we should concentrate our efforts, especially given it was likely to be eschewed by other organisations more recently arrived. It seemed water, food and medical care were the greatest needs and we began discussing how we could provide these in Cité Soleil. We recognised that the Hands Together school compounds, with their high surrounding walls, could possibly become the secure bases from which we could work and safely distribute emergency aid. We decided to go and assess that possibility ourselves.

As we drove through Cité Soleil, life did not seem dramatically different, although the people crowded around us and told us of their needs and asked us for help even more urgently than normal. But when we got to the first school our hearts sank. The perimeter walls had collapsed, along with some of the classrooms. Huge cracks ran through the walls that were still standing – and through concrete playgrounds too. For the first time I saw our co-workers, very hardened men who had grown up here among the gangs of Cité Soleil, break down and weep. I realised more than ever before that these schools were the most powerful symbols of hope in this community. They were a source of great pride too. Some of the men in tears had worked on their construction and some helped run them. To see them in ruins was too much and the dam that had been holding back their grief collapsed. But soon they had wiped away their tears and resumed the discussion of practicalities – pointing out that the blocks of the toppled perimeter wall could be reused to reconstruct them very quickly, and thus we would have our secure base. They began debating whether the school could be repaired or whether it would need to be pulled down – most were optimistic about repair. We continued on to the next school, and then the next, where children who should have been in class played amid the rubble while we assessed the damage.

Having inspected all the schools, we finally arrived back to find a hive of activity at Father Tom's little compound. Already a group of men were rebuilding a collapsed wall to make our space secure once again; some ladies were cooking a pot of rice, while nearby the Hands Together water tanker truck was filling up (even in the best of times this vehicle took clean water into Cité Soleil each day on a regular basis for people to fill their buckets and bottles). We sat down for another meeting with teachers and community leaders who, like most here, had been living on the streets since the earthquake. Various teams were formed with immediate tasks. One was to begin making an immediate assessment of each school community. Who had died? Who had lost their house? What was each family's current situation? Another team was to begin picking out the reusable bricks from the debris around each school.

As we talked further it dawned on us that unless we could secure a supply of fuel, all our other plans would become futile. Doug and I decided to head immediately to the UN compound, where various organisations seemed to be making their base, in order to try to secure some of that vital commodity.

It had already been a long day when we arrived at the UN base. We entered a reception area and explained our urgent request to the man at the counter. We were directed to another office and then another, explaining our situation anew each time and pleading for some fuel. Nobody disputed the legitimacy of our request, or the fact that they had a large supply available for this purpose, but none was willing to take responsibility for giving us what we needed. Eventually, an earnest young man pointed at a large tent and suggested we try it, explaining that there was a meeting of various international NGOs taking place there. We slipped in quietly at the back of a meeting that was already under way. I looked around at a tent full of white people. A wide variety of accented English was being spoken from all over the world, but there was not one black face in the crowded tent. I couldn't help but make the comparison with the meeting we had just left in Father Tom's yard. It became clear from the discussion that most had only just arrived in Haiti.

A man stood up and introduced himself as belonging to a well-known global aid organisation. He began to complain at great length about the poor accommodation that he and his colleagues had been provided with. He was indignant about this and some others began to raise their voices in support of him. Doug and I looked at each other. I could see the anger rise in his face and I was concerned about what he might do in his state of exhaustion and post-traumatic stress. I was relieved when he simply walked out of the tent, leaving behind a lively debate about the deficiencies of the sleeping quarters. Without saying a word to each other, we marched straight back past the offices and into the warehouse where we could see an enormous stack of barrels. We told the startled man in the stock room that we needed one barrel immediately, and could he please have it placed in the back of our pick-up straight away as we were in a very big hurry. I think the pent-up fury, borne of our experience in the tent, must have been plainly evident in our faces. He didn't even ask a question, let alone put up an argument, and a few minutes later we were heading back through the pitiful streets with our precious cargo, passing thousands of hungry, injured people who really would have had a reason to complain about substandard accommodation if there had been anyone to listen.

That experience in the tent with the international NGOs was the first thing I thought of when, eight years later, I began reading about an emerging scandal centred on the behaviour of some staff working for foreign aid organisations in the aftermath of the earthquake. On 9 February 2018 *The Times*' front-page headline read: 'Top Oxfam workers paid Haiti survivors for sex'. The article also alleged that Oxfam covered up the claims that senior staff working in Haiti in the wake of the 2010 earthquake used prostitutes, some of whom may have been under age. Two days later a follow-up article in *The Times* reported new claims that more than 120 workers from UK charities had been accused of sexual abuse in the last year. A series of revelations and allegations emerged in the following days and weeks. The UK government's Department for International Development cut all funding to Oxfam – previously one of the biggest recipients – and the government of Haiti later banned the organisation from working in their country ever again. They explained that they took this decision because of the 'violation of its laws and serious breach of the principle of human dignity'.

The impact of all this was not only felt by Oxfam but sent shudders through every charity working in international development. The media pressed each aid organisation to make public any cases of sexual misconduct and a plethora of other such cases emerged, dragging many others into the scandal. Some experienced significant decreases in support. The reputation of the international aid sector was further tarnished. And charity was in the dock once again.

3

Organising Love

... when all violence subsides in the human heart,
the state which remains is love. It is not something
we have to acquire; it is always present and needs
only to be uncovered. This is our real nature, not
merely to love one person here, another there,
but to be love itself.

MAHATMA GANDHI

When we feel bruised and battered by events – like the scandalous things that took place in Haiti or other mistakes of our own making – we need, first of all, to remind ourselves why: why are we doing this? Why is our charity so precious and so needed? We need to convince ourselves once again that the risk is worth taking. Because, make no mistake, every authentic act of charity – whether we make it as individuals or as an organisation – involves an element of risk: the risk of our gift being misused by the homeless person or the charity we donate to; the risk that the project we support does not, in the end, manage to solve the problems it set out to solve;

the risk that our charity's reputation is torn to shreds by the misdemeanours of a member of our staff; the risk that one day we will not be able to raise the funds required to keep our precious project afloat and end up breaking our promises to vulnerable people. Such risks, along with our own mistakes and the criticisms we receive – both constructive and destructive – will require us to remind ourselves why. At times of crisis and disenchantment – and at many other times too, even before we attempt to learn from our mistakes and chart a way forward – we need to remind ourselves why. Why did we set out on this journey? Why should we keep going? We cannot ask these questions too often in our pursuit of charity.

Malawi, June 2016

Yamakani is sitting at the back of her thatched mud-brick cottage with her two younger brothers, Amos, ten, and Promise, four. When their grandfather died earlier this year, she became the head of her family at twelve years old. Little Promise snuggles beside Yamakani as she points at their little parched field sloping away from their home in the village of Chigona, set on a high ridge with vast, spectacular vistas in each direction. The tumbling blue hills of Mozambique can be seen in the distance, one fading shade of blue behind another, like an exquisite colour chart. If beauty could be bottled and sold the people here would not be hungry and desperate, but even before this current drought, this little child-headed family was heavily burdened by a struggle for survival.

Yamakani tries to explain to us how hard their lives have been since their grandfather died, and how it has become even harder since their harvest failed:

'This year we didn't even harvest one whole bag of maize. We finished eating that a few weeks ago. Now, after school we go into other people's fields to look for any little bits of maize that might have been left behind after the harvest. But we are finding very little now.'

Given the desperation in every household here I am surprised that they have found any at all. Amos looks up at a large tree beside their home and tells us that it bears precious fruit, but then explains that they need to be very careful because snakes live in the branches.

'They are very dangerous, so we stand back from it and throw stones to try and knock the fruit down,' he tells us.

And then he expounds, with a glimmer of pride, on their plan to try to dry the fruit on their roof so it might last for the coming months. If it wasn't for the very evident reality of their grim plight they would have sounded like children everywhere who hatch wonderful plans and play at being adults.

'Very often now the porridge that Mary's Meals provides at our school is our only proper meal of the day,' Yamakani explains.

'We never eat before school, and often there is nothing in the evening so we go to bed hungry. We have exams right now. It is difficult for us to study because after school we have to look for food and we don't have any light in the house when it gets dark. But the exams are the most important thing because I would like to be a nurse – a midwife,' smiles

Yamakani, as her little brother, Promise, clambers on to her lap.

For a whole week we traverse the southern region of a hungry country that is suffering an El-Niño-induced drought, visiting family after desperate family. Outside Lucia Tiedze's home a small quantity of nuts are spread on a grubby old sack. They are large, the size of golf balls, and unfamiliar to me. Lucia insists on breaking one open – despite us asking her not to – to reveal the disappointingly small inner flesh within the thick layers of inedible shell.

'I collect these from the forest,' she explains. 'They are the only food I have had this week.'

She is the mother of six children and her second son, Chimuza, a handsome bright-eyed fourteen-year-old, sits beside her outside their home in Mchenga, a small village on the hot flat plains of Chikwawa. At near sea level, this area is the lowest point in Malawi. Even now, in midwinter, it is hot. Earlier this year unprecedented floods submerged much of the plain. The Shire and other rivers roared down the escarpment, carrying the rain that had fallen in record-breaking quantities, washing away homes and crops and the things people depend on for life. Today the large cracks that run through the mud-brick walls of some homes are the only signs left of that deluge and it is hard to imagine it happened at all. For in the months since, the flat lands of Chikwawa have become an enormous dustbowl as Malawi experiences its driest year for thirty-five years.

'This year we only harvested one bag of maize from our field and we have already finished that. Our only hope is to try and get "piece work" (casual labour) but there is very little now.

Sometimes we go to work together as a whole family on someone else's field. We earn 500 kwacha (60p) for a day's work,' Lucia explains patiently.

I have often enjoyed visiting Malawi at this time of year, the season of plenty when, post-harvest, maize stores and children's tummies are full and the smallholder farmers of Malawi enjoy a period of welcome respite from their relentless struggle with hunger. This year is shockingly different. The plight of this small land-locked country, which has already sunk to very near the bottom of the list of the world's poorest nations in recent years, seems to have reached a new low.

'There is hunger roaming around,' says Malita, one of Lucia's neighbours, who explains her husband is away collecting reeds which he uses to weave mats like the one she invites us to sit on at her door.

'It takes him a whole day to make one and he can sell them at the local market for about 500 kwacha. We sell about three of them every week. We have a field in which we grow sorghum and cotton, but this year, because of too much sun, we produced nothing at all.'

Chimuza makes it clear he would like to change the subject from their desperate search for food. His mother, Lucia, explains proudly that he is the highest-scoring student in the village school.

'I want to be a doctor so the people around here can get help more quickly at the hospital.'

His sparking face and excitement lifts all of us and it is easy to believe he has the talent to be a doctor. But then his eyes are drawn back to the pile of nuts on the sack.

'I am worried about the hunger, though. I am worried about my little brothers and sisters because they get very weak. What are we going to do? I wish a good life for my brothers and sisters. I enjoy learning. I have an English exam tomorrow.'

'But I am scared we might die. I am afraid the hunger might kill us.'

Yamakani and Chimuza are the reason why charities like ourselves keep going.

That it is possible to help people living far away from us is one of the wonderful opportunities of our era, especially given that this age is also one marked by a ghastly disparity between the richest and poorest parts of our world. The desire of those who have more than they need to share with people who do not have even the most basic things is one that grows in many hearts. And when we wish to go back to basics and remind ourselves why we do this, it can also be important to remind ourselves of that appalling gap between our wealth and those who have nothing.

And we might also at times need to remind ourselves just how wealthy we are. You, yourself, dear reader, are probably a very rich person. Maybe even richer than you know. If you earn even the minimum wage in the UK, you are among the richest 4 per cent of people in the world, and if you earn the average salary for a registered nurse in the UK, you are comfortably among the wealthiest 1 per cent on the planet. About half of the wealth in the world is owned by that 1 per cent. But that elite – the 1 per cent – are not the people who appear in the newspapers' 'Rich Lists'. They are most likely you and me.

Those of us whose biggest concerns are our mortgage, our career progression, the deficiencies of our children's schools, healthy eating and pension provision may find it difficult – even if we wanted to – to forget the millions who are instead preoccupied by the fact they have no house to live in, no paid work, no possibility that their children will learn to read and write, no food to serve their children in the morning and no thought of a retirement plan, aside from a hope that some of their children might be still be living and able to take care of them in the unlikely event that they reach old age themselves. And we are even more likely to want to share a little of what we own when we understand that just a miniscule amount of sharing can transform the lives of children like Yamakani and Chimuza. For those who make up the poorest 10 per cent of people on Earth need to work for eleven days to earn as much as that registered nurse in the UK earns in just one hour. The choice by someone to share even part of what they earn in an hour can change a life – even save a life.

Iowa, Autumn 2014

A large man with a weathered face approached me from the crowd as I stood at our stall during the Christ Our Life Conference in Des Moines, Iowa. He shook my hand and reminded me that he had spoken to me at this same event the previous year.

'I just wanted to let you know, that after learning about Mary's Meals last year, I made a decision. A few years back, I gave up doing overtime. I'm a construction worker. It's hard work at my age and I don't really need the extra income any more. Anyhow, I decided last year to start doing the overtime again. I kept all my earnings from that aside for your charity. Here they are – for the hungry children.'

He handed me a substantial cheque. I looked up at him and noticed his eyes were brimming with tears.

'Thank you,' he said (before I could), wiping his eyes.

'I'm going to keep doing it!' he called back to me over his shoulder as he strode away.

Czech Republic, Summer 2018

Apricot dumplings. I am still not sure I like them. I had never even heard of them before, but now I was faced with several large ones on my lunch plate. It was my first day in the Czech Republic and I was receiving a very warm welcome from my hosts, who had met me at the airport and provided me with much interesting information about their homeland on our drive. I was pleased to learn that *pivo* was their word for beer, just as it is in Croatia and Bosnia–Herzegovina, where the summers are long and hot and where I have, on occasion, been forced to quaff one or two. The easy learning of this word made me happy, both because of the familiarity of it and because it made me feel comfortable with these strangers in a strange land, whose priorities in teaching me the first essential phrases of their language aligned closely with my own.

They were a group of volunteers who had founded Mary's Meals in the Czech Republic and who I had therefore heard quite a lot about. I was intrigued by them because support for our mission in a country where, until a few months ago, few had heard of us was growing incredibly rapidly. For some time I had been looking forward to understanding why and how.

Lucy and Karel, along with their friend Marian, were the couple who had taken it upon themselves to begin our work here, and in their family home – a modest apartment in the city of Brno – I was given a seat at their dining room table and served the apricot dumplings: a Czech speciality, I learnt. I am still not absolutely sure whether I like them, even now, because that day I was feeling a little unwell, suffering some kind of migraine thing that was making me a little nauseous. But I didn't want to offend my hosts by failing to devour the dumplings – several of them the size of tennis balls.

Over lunch they ran through our itinerary for my short visit and advised me on the talk I was to give at the Christian conference in the town the next day, explaining that 8,000 people would be there. My nerves added to my struggle with the apricot dumplings, which now appeared to be the size of footballs rather than tennis balls.

I then tried to turn the conversation towards finding out about Lucy, Karel and Marian. They were a little reluctant at first to talk about themselves and what had led them to initiate the mission of Mary's Meals in their country, but I persevered.

Lucy and Karel were owners of a business – an estate agency. It had been doing well and they were moving towards realising their dream of building a new family home for themselves and their eighteen-month-old son, Samuel, who was playing quietly with his toys in the corner. They had bought the land and had house plans drawn up. They spread the architect's drawings on the floor in front us and I could see that what was being designed was indeed a dream home.

Then they explained that about one year previously a friend had given them a copy of my book, *The Shed That Fed a Million Children*, which had just been translated into Czech. The reading of it prompted a new conversation between them.

'Do we really need a new house? Don't we already have everything we really need?' they asked each other.

After several conversations, they eventually came to a decision to scrap their plans for a new home, which were by then at a very advanced stage. Instead they would use the funds they had been saving as a donation to found Mary's Meals in the Czech Republic and thus cover all its start-up costs.

'Marian did the same!' they said, pointing at their embarrassed friend sitting at the table. 'He sold his land too and added this to the funds for Mary's Meals,' they exclaimed, happy to deflect the conversation as quickly as possible from their own extraordinary act of giving.

By now I was desperately searching for words. I was overcome by the goodness of these people and the enormity of their self-sacrificial act. And now they were thanking me for the opportunity to be part of this mission. The desire to be the best possible steward of such a gift rose again in my heart but I felt very small and inadequate in the face of this startling charity.

I was happy to be distracted by the gurgling of little Samuel beside me. I looked down at him as he held up a toy house triumphantly. We all began laughing and, as we did, I realised that it wasn't really a toy house at all. It was an architect's model, of the dream house that he would never now live in.

He was too young to know that of course; too young to realise his parents would bequeath him something much greater.

Lucy, Karel, Marian and the man in Iowa are also the reason why. They cannot invite Yamakani and Chimuza to dine with them in their home in Brno, or hand them money at a stall in Iowa. That is why an organisation like Mary's Meals exists; to enable those who wish to share some of what they have with those who lack even the basics of life in as effective a way as possible. I have been embarrassed many times by people who thank us profusely when they are making a gift to Mary's Meals – and it seems that often, those who give in the most extraordinary ways are the most likely to express the most profound gratitude. But I have begun to understand why. They are the ones whose burning compassion most urgently needs to find an outlet – a way of transforming their love into a real, practical act of charity. When they thank us, even before we have been able to thank them, they do so with absolute sincerity because we have helped them fulfil a very deeply held desire. And so, when it happens now, I do not feel embarrassment as much as an enormous sense of responsibility for ensuring that all that kindness does indeed become effective help for the people it seeks to help.

This is why our tiny informal effort in 1992 to transport gifts from generous people in Scotland to those suffering in refugee camps in Bosnia–Herzegovina became, unexpectedly, an ongoing mission filled with so much joy. We inadvertently tapped into an incredibly rich seam of heroic goodness, one that pre-existed our little appeal. That appeal prompted a stream of giving that seemed impossible to stop even if we had wished it to, while at the same time, the great suffering of people in the disintegrating Yugoslavia cried out for that torrent of goodness to reach them. In many ways, that has been the recurring story of our organisation ever since. I feel that our job as a charity has been a bit like that of a water engineer, trying to ensure that a great store of water flows, without leakage or contamination, to where people need it. As the stream has grown into a mighty river, we have had to become experts at building banks and dams to prevent floods in the wrong places at the wrong times. We have had to construct canals as we become aware of new sources of water and new places where people thirst for it. We have had to find ways to filter it and keep it pure until it reaches the parched lands it seeks.

We are not the water itself though. And we certainly never made it. We are only the stewards entrusted with it. It is crucial we do not become confused about that, lest we who work for charitable organisations eventually end up thinking we can walk on the stuff.

And in my own experience, the projects that are most successful and most beautiful are the ones built on good deeds already taking place. They work simply by providing the resources required for such love to be more effective and by putting an organisational frame around it – only enough to allow those acts to grow and bear fruit, not so much that it stifles and shuts out the light they need to grow and flourish.

* * *

Once upon a time in Transylvania, in a town called Târgu Mureș, there was a small group of local volunteers so full of love that they disregarded two deeply held prejudices of their community: disdain of the Roma and the stigma of HIV/ AIDS. They embraced both of those scandalous things at once by visiting children of that despised community who had been abandoned in a local hospital after being diagnosed as HIV positive (they had been infected by contaminated blood supplies during basic hospital procedures). The time they spent with those lonely, sick children – some of them unable to walk at eleven years of age because they had never been lifted out of their cots for long enough for them to learn – led to a dream of rescuing them from the dim, loveless hospital, where they were condemned to die sooner rather than later. We began working with those volunteers to realise that dream, matching their love with that of donors in faraway lands in order to build three family-style homes. In time, every child from that ward still living was given a new life where they were wrapped in the love of local carers (including some of those original volunteers who gave up good jobs to dedicate themselves to looking after those little ones).

When we built those homes we expected them to be hospices. Our hope was that these children would, at least, experience love and a dignified death. But they became something else – a place where most of the children didn't die, but instead grew into adulthood. Since then I have attended the weddings of three girls who we had first encountered as emaciated, disturbed children condemned to die in their cots. Instead I saw them, beautiful and beaming, dancing in their new husbands' arms. They have since become mothers of healthy, bouncing babies. None of that would have happened without those volunteers who gave up a little time to visit some lonely children who no one else wanted to know. That whole amazing story has been built on their love.

Sometimes, even when we have thought we were leading the way with a new project, we have discovered that spontaneous charity has beaten us to it. And that has been good – a reminder that our role is only to steward that charity in a way that lets it flourish and grow and bear all sorts of fruit.

In the late 1990s, towards the end of one of Liberia's civil wars, we began to accompany some of the Gola people, returning from years of exile in displaced camps, back to their villages in Bomi County. There they discovered that their homes were now overgrown ruins and that there was a new forest growing where their fields used to be. We tried to help them in various ways by providing machetes for them to clear the encroaching bush, tools to start rebuilding homes and food supplies until they could start growing and harvesting their own crops once again. In addition, we supported a mobile health clinic which began to serve remote villages with a team of local nurses and cases of medicines. Each Tuesday we visited Massetin, a leper colony where the people had been suffering terribly without any healthcare for many years during the war. Unlike the surrounding villages, Massetin had largely been left alone by the warring soldiers, whose terror of contracting leprosy led to them giving the place a wide berth, and therefore the people here had stayed while other villages emptied.

In Massetin we came to know a young man called Massaquoi and learnt his story. He had had to flee for his life from his own home village during the war. Eventually, as he stole in terror through the thick forest, he came by chance upon Massetin. He decided to stay there and began to tend to the lepers, who were at that time living in desperation. When the war ended he never left, continuing to help them as best he could. He was overjoyed when our clinic began to visit, and in time we provided him with training so that he could become a key member of our team.

We thought our little clinic was a particularly intrepid initiative, helping people in places far beyond the reach of other organised help. But of course, we discovered in Massetin that long before we arrived, charity was already at work and that, in the form of Massaquoi, heroic goodness was alive and well and ready to become part of something more organised.

Experiences like that have left me feeling that it is a little odd that an organisation like ours is called 'a charity'. We are a body established with the purpose of encouraging and making effective the acts of charity performed by individual people. We are not charity itself. Organisations do not perform acts of charity – individual human beings do. It is certainly possible, and expected, that the individuals who comprise an organisation like ours carry out acts of charity, but it is equally possible to work for a charity and not practise it. I can certainly be guilty of that. I do not want to get stuck here on semantics, nor am I proposing a change to a long-established terminology which I use myself, I raise it only because I feel it might correspond to certain wrong attitudes we can adopt when working for a charity. There can be a tendency to think we are 'in charge' in the wrong way, or even that we are the prime movers, when – certainly in the case of a grassroots movement like Mary's Meals – we are the servants of people's goodness rather than the leaders of it: we are enablers rather than key actors; we are joiners of dots rather than creative geniuses; and we are stewards rather than owners.

Charity is love. Organisations cannot love people. Loving is something that only God and humans can do. Charitable organisations exist to enable people to do so more effectively.

Having said all that, it is a great honour and privilege to work for an organisation that is put in a category with such a magnificent label. To work for charity! What a wonderful boss to have! And the truth is that there have been occasions during our own development as an organisation when I have, during internal debate, stoutly defended our use of this designation. The challenge to its use stemmed not from the concerns I have expressed above, but for other interesting and important reasons of identity that we will revisit as we journey on.

So, while individual goodness and charity live in every hidden corner of the Earth, sooner or later, in the face of large-scale and endemic human suffering, in order to be effective in relieving it things need to become organised. An authentic charity desires this, because it wants to be as effective as it can possibly be. Becoming organised is also essential in allowing people in places separated by great distances to help each other. And so, in order to express our love effectively and to reach even those in distant lands, charitable organisations are born. We do not always have the opportunity to sit down on a park bench beside the one who needs our help. We cannot invite all who are without water to pop round and fill up at our tap. We cannot serve with our own hands, no matter how much we would love to, a good meal to a starving child living on a distant continent. And, please God, we will never find ourselves so close to someone who has been buried by an earthquake that we can speak them words of comfort.

The airing of those disgraceful things done in the name of charity after the 2010 earthquake in Haiti was certainly a good thing even if the press coverage did, quite blatantly in some cases, become hijacked by an anti-overseas-aid agenda. It shone a light on wickedness that wished to cower in the dark and thus provided a crucial service to all those millions of people around the world engaging in authentic acts of charity, and to all those whose desperate vulnerability leaves them at risk of exploitation.

In the short term, the publicity and scrutiny prompted all of us with responsibilities in aid organisations to thoroughly review our policies relating to child protection and sexual misconduct, and to ask ourselves if there was anything else we could do to make them more robust. The scandal provoked more fundamental questions too. Some used the debate as an opportunity to attack the wisdom of overseas aid itself.

'Look, I told you so!' cried some voices, before calling governments to reduce or scrap their budgets for foreign aid. Others focused on a more legitimate target, the organisations themselves. While in most cases this may not have been justified, at least, guilty or not, the correct defendants (the organisations using her name rather than charity itself) were now on trial. Unfortunately this episode and others like it tarnished not just specific organisations but charities in general, confirming some people's view that charities are all corrupt organisations, oozing with hypocrisy and unworthy of support. That wasn't helped when it appeared that some in those organisations seemed unable to accept that enormous wrong had happened.

Some argue that such things will just inevitably happen from time to time in organisations employing thousands of staff all over the world – 'a few bad apples' and all that. They can even be legitimised and excused: 'What do you expect when men are working far away from home for months on end in stressful circumstances?' Or 'these things happen in every society and always have'.

While it would be reasonable to consider the prevalence of such incidents against the scale of the organisations involved and to recognise the truly enormous amount of good an organisation like Oxfam has done – and will continue to do – in so many of the world's poorest nations, no one should ever try to excuse or justify the behaviour that caused this scandal in Haiti. Deeds like these are inexcusable and unjustifiable. Always. The exploitation of vulnerable women and the abuse of children are evil things, wherever and whenever they happen. They are the antithesis of charity and it is grotesque that they could be carried out by people sheltering under her name. The fact that foul things like that happen in every society, and always have, is irrelevant. Those specific events in Haiti happened in very particular circumstances and were carried out by men who would not have been in a position to act in that way (they would not have even been in the country) if they had not been deployed there by charitable organisations and given enormous power. Those of us with responsibility for any aspect of this have a weighty responsibility indeed, and one that goes beyond very necessary things such as policies relating to child protection, a strategy for recruiting staff, the sharing of information between charities and a plan for reporting and communicating with supporters and press when something does go wrong. While all those good things are indeed essential, they should not be confused with the task of getting to the roots of how such depraved behaviour could ever happen under the guise of charity.

There may be a risk in making a link between the merely arrogant and insensitive behaviour which incensed Doug and I in that tent after the earthquake and the much more sinister and, indeed, criminal behaviour later exposed, but I think there is one.

This kind of work is inherently dangerous. No matter how hard we strive to mitigate the risks, all of us involved in leading charitable organisations know that decades of hard work by good people can be undermined by the wicked actions of one individual. None of us can say with absolute certainty it could never happen in our organisation, even as we strain every sinew to try to ensure it doesn't. None of us can claim we have all the answers. And we cannot let these terrible incidents completely overshadow the enormous good the organisations caught up in these scandals continue to do.

However, I make the link between these events because I believe that when people who work in the name of charity stop respecting those they serve, things will, inevitably, go wrong. When that attitude becomes one of blatant disrespect, like that which we witnessed in that tent, then it is going to go wrong, horribly, sooner rather than later. The work required within an organisation to try to prevent this from ever happening is a comprehensive one and needs to begin a long time before those people ever gather in a tent in a foreign land in the aftermath of a disaster – and it is a work that needs to continue every day for as long as the organisation exists.

The giving of aid to those in desperate need creates, for the giver, enormous power. I thought about this for the first time when I began delivering donated aid to refugees in the former Yugoslavia. I became aware that I was starting to think of myself as important and even superior to the destitute people so dependent on what we were distributing to them. As I made friends with some of those in the camps, I couldn't avoid the absurdity of this temptation, because it became clear that many of them were much better educated than me, had had a richer experience of life and had enjoyed greater 'success' in a variety of ways. It just so happened that they needed our help at that moment in time. But the notion that this made me superior couldn't withstand even the most casual scrutiny, thankfully. What's more, the aid I was unloading out of the back of my truck wasn't even mine. Those gifts in my lorry were there only because some immensely kind people back in Scotland were sharing some of their belongings with these people. They were the givers. I was just a truck driver – and even the truck itself was a gift!

I began to recognise one of the great perils of working for a charity and to understand that if those tendencies towards feelings of superiority and disrespect are not deliberately counteracted, they will eventually destroy all that might have been good in the first place. It was by making friends with those in the camps that I began to see that great danger. I came to know them as individual people, not as labelled groups: 'refugees', 'internally displaced people', 'beneficiaries'. The fact that we were – in the days I describe – a tiny organisation, working very directly with those we were trying to help, had the huge advantage of allowing us to form relationships with those we served. But that changes as organisations grow. The aloofness of many large aid agencies can become their fatal flaw. When those bringing help live in compounds behind barbed wire, from which they emerge in shiny four-wheel-drive vehicles only to frequent expensive hotels and restaurants, the already huge chasm between the giver and the receiver becomes an unbridgeable abyss. Gradually, and subtly, the attitude of the once-idealistic aid worker can change. The poor who we once loved and respected can start to become in our minds the problem rather than the solution, especially in times of frustration and failure. We forget that it is the poor, rather than ourselves, who will play the leading role in setting their communities free. In our ivory towers we can slip very easily towards having the attitude of a saviour rather than a servant. And that is a momentous mistake to make.

There is a danger in oversimplifying these matters. Security concerns, cultural differences and the challenge of recruiting staff with specialised skills to work in very difficult locations often mean that safe, comfortable accommodation detached from the local community needs to be provided. The provision of robust, reliable vehicles can also be essential when working in the face of security risks and the absence of smooth roads. A desire to live like the local population can become an unrealistic, romantic one which, if insisted upon, might place a new burden on an already heavily burdened community. These are not easy judgements. Compromises between the ideal and the pragmatic will most often have to be made. However, that does not mean that those of us responsible should ever stop confronting these issues – no matter how uncomfortable they make us feel – and be willing to make decisions that may challenge the norm. For example, in order to work effectively in certain circumstances, it will sometimes be necessary to buy a large, expensive four-wheel-drive vehicle. It would not be possible to deliver goods to villages miles from a tarred road without one. However, fleets of such vehicles, owned by NGOs and UN bodies, clog the already congested streets of every major city in the developing world. I suspect many such vehicles rarely leave a tarred road, but somehow they seem to have become de rigueur for aid organisation staff, who could just as easily be moving from meeting to meeting in a small car, or maybe even on a bicycle. Not only would this save cost (and help save the planet), it would create new possibilities of building bridges across the treacherous ravines that separate givers and receivers.

A certain NGO culture (intertwined with that of the UN and other international bodies) seems to exist in the world's poorest countries. And, of course, some kind of distinct culture is bound to form among groups of people living very far from home engaged in a particular type of work in often challenging circumstances. But sometimes it appears that culture has evolved from, or even replaced, the cultures of colonialism, when people chose to 'serve the Empire' by working in distant lands, motivated largely by the new lifestyle this afforded them. Hearing those voices in the tent talking about the standard of their own accommodation and expressing outrage that it wasn't up to scratch sounded to me very much like the sentiments of an entitled society. And that is certainly not the only time I have heard such voices.

This risk, of setting ourselves apart from those we serve, does not only afflict us when we are working in places of abject poverty. It also happens when people like me forget that the gifts in the truck are not mine and that I am entrusted with their good stewardship only. Those of us privileged to be able to call charity our boss also need to recognise that, in a certain way, those givers, those 'doers of charity', are also our bosses. Ultimately, they are our employers. Without their freely given support and startling acts of charity, many of our organisations simply wouldn't exist. It is possible for us to lose respect for those supporters, just as it is possible for us to do the same with their brothers and sisters in the developing world. We can do this by dehumanising them; by treating them like ATM machines from which we extract as much cash as possible, or by employing certain marketing techniques. Their giving patterns and potential to give more are analysed until they are not people any more – just statistics and graphs. We risk imprisoning ourselves in offices, working ferociously with our computers and failing to interact, ever, with the people who brought our work into existence.

And we are the poorer for it. When we refuse to get out of the big jeep and walk with the people by the side of a dusty road, or we disdain the idea of sitting down at a coffee morning held in support of our mission to befriend volunteers with big hearts and small bank accounts, ultimately we are the losers, the people who are missing a great opportunity to learn how to be more fully human.

If allowed to fester unchecked, this separation from and disrespect for our supporters will eventually lead to disdain – often in the form of a superiority that sees donors as irksome, simplistic people to be tolerated and fundraising as a necessary evil, only carried out in order to do our 'real work' on the other side of the world. To think that way is to miss, in a tragic way, the beauty of charity. When we bring our cause to someone, hoping for their support, we do not do so in a spirit of trying to take something from them. We are doing something quite the opposite. When they decide to give something to our organisation, and thus make a gift to the one in need, they are not diminished by that choice; rather they become more fully human, more joyful.

These are just some of the huge inherent challenges in organising charity. Recognising the very great danger of taking a wrong turning on the road as we gallop onwards is one thing. Finding a safe way to navigate our route correctly in all circumstances is quite another, especially because often the route we should take is the less-travelled path, through a narrow gate, lacking even a decent signpost and even easier to miss when it gets dark! Our best chance at that point is to know the stars and the art of using them to guide us.

It is essential that every charitable organisation develops a set of organisational values that can be those stars. To plot a safe course, we need to know them and use them as our reference point in all circumstances. Our vision (the pole star) and our values need to be shared by all in the mission and deeply embedded in those with positions of responsibility. This does not happen by having a brain-storming session one day, listing a set of statements with lots of fashionable words and then putting them away in a file, only to reappear from time to time at board meetings. Charity work is too dangerous, and the wrong turnings too hard to differentiate from the right turnings, to take that approach. To serve charity in a way that is worthy of the name requires us to be organisations who put our values first; ahead of monetary targets, short-term goals and a desire to become the biggest, the best known, the most impressive. Our values, if we devote time to articulating them thoughtfully, will enable us to understand fully our own unique mission and appreciate more deeply the beauty of it. It will help us avoid the mistake of thinking we need to become like other, more established organisations, and instead strive to become the very best version of our own unique mission (in this regard charities are just like people). If we are brave enough and stubborn enough to ensure all who join our mission know, understand and share these values, then we will create a security and confidence that allows all of us to move forward together, under the light of those stars, knowing how to get up and continue on towards the ones we serve, even after we make a mistake and fall flat on our face in the ditch.

And, make no mistake, each one of us, in serious pursuit of charity, will fall on our faces sooner or later. Because, without exception, every time we choose to perform an act of charity, we choose to take a risk.

Glasgow, Winter 2018

My nephew, Joe, and my son, Calum, both in their twenties, share a flat in Glasgow. One evening when Calum got home Joe was bent under the kitchen sink trying to fix their leaky waste pipe.

'Oh, Calum, I invited a homeless guy back to borrow our shower. He's in there now – Eastern European, Romanian, maybe – very little English ...'

As Joe spoke a gush of water exploded from under the sink, soaking him, and quickly began to pour on to the kitchen floor. By now the freshly showered stranger had appeared with a towel over his shoulder, talking to them loudly and urgently in what sounded like a mixture of Spanish and French.

'It's OK. Don't worry at all. We'll fix it,' Joe said to him, not having understood a word, but trying to sound calm, as he and Calum disappeared under the sink again. But the water kept spurting out. Their prolonged, fruitless efforts became desperate.

'Arrrgh!! I wish I had smaller hands! I just cannot get in to tighten that thing,' Calum screamed from under the sink, abandoning all pretence that they had the situation under control.

Their guest, sitting on the sofa, began yelling more frantically now, gesticulating wildly as he fired a cascade of unintelligible words towards them.

'Look. It's OK. Better you just leave,' Joe said to the man, having long stopped trying to figure out what he was saying and gesturing towards the door, to ensure that he understood he was now overstaying his welcome.

As the man made for the exit, Joe's sister walked into the scene of watery chaos.

'Jessica! You speak French, don't you?' the boys shouted together.

The man addressed Jessica with his message, shouting and waving his arms like a mad man.

'Ah! You are a plumber,' replied Jessica. "And you know how to fix that.'

By now the man's footsteps were echoing down their stair-well and the door to the street slammed behind him.

'His hands were tiny too,' Calum observed later.

4

The Heart and the Head

A fool with a heart and no sense is just as unhappy
as a fool with sense and no heart.

FYODOR DOSTOEVSKY

Part One (The Heart)

Why are we so prone to making mistakes in the practice of
charity? Learning to play even her most basic notes involves
sweat and tears for some of us, while even the more talented
can but dream of ever becoming a virtuoso. The reasons that
cause us to go off course in our pursuit of charity are many, but
most have their roots in the same grave error; that of allowing
love and truth to become separated.

When love and truth divorce, charity will quickly mutate
into something else. If the head becomes disconnected from
the heart, before too long both occupy only a corpse. Charity,
it seems, begins in our hearts; those spontaneous feelings of
compassion which prompt us to want to do something good
for the suffering person. But for a charitable act to happen,

those feelings need to invite our brain to figure out what exactly we should do, and then how we should do it. The screams of someone trapped beneath a pile of concrete move us to want to help, but then we need to assess the best way to do that. How can we quickly move several tonnes of rubble? Or, if that seems impossible, in what other way might we help the suffering person? In responding to a one-off emergency this is a relatively straightforward process; a clearly signposted short journey from heart to head. However, for ongoing, co-ordinated missions that go beyond impulsive unstructured deeds, things can get a little more convoluted.

I have seen many a war waged between the head and the heart. Some have been civil wars: the struggle within a person as they try to balance the love that initially hurled them off on the journey with the required professional skills and structures that might be required to sustain it. Others have been conflicts fought between factions within growing organisations – one side throwing up defences around the heart and the origins of their beloved charity, using phrases like 'founding values' and 'the spirit of the work', while the other launches raids with weapons such as 'accountability', 'proof of impact' and 'strategic growth plans'. Like all wars, these are stupid, sad things. Healthy works of charity can only grow and flourish when the impulses of the heart (love) and the guidance of the head (truth) are both held in the deepest respect and understood as essential. A certain tension will inevitably exist between these two great forces, but if this can be held, with each resisting the temptation to overpower the other, the most beautiful works of charity can thrive. But the temptation to ignore the heart or dismiss the head is a powerful one.

We can forget love so easily. We might think we've 'grown out of that stage'. Or perhaps our hearts are just not big enough yet to meet every situation with love. I once learnt a lesson about that during a stupid, sad war (which sadly wasn't metaphorical).

I spent most of 1993 driving truck-loads of donated aid from Scotland to people suffering during the prolonged violent death of Yugoslavia. On each trip I was accompanied by a co-driver, very often a member of my own family. On one mission to bring medical aid to an institution caring for children with special needs near the city of Zadar, in Croatia, my father volunteered to come with me. After four days of driving, we finally began unloading boxes of vital supplies in the courtyard of the hospital, which was at that stage very near the front line – a fact that became all too apparent when some shells exploded uncomfortably close to where we were working. The nurses who were helping us unload had already spoken to us about their terror of the approaching front line and the thought of trying to flee with children who were unable to walk and who needed constant care and support. They urged us to finish our unloading as quickly as possible and head north to safety. Not needing much persuasion to do just that, I hurriedly passed the last box from the back of the truck and jumped into the driver's seat. I revved the engine and wondered what was keeping my dad. Impatiently I looked in my rear-view mirror and saw him speaking to the nurses and staff and giving them each a big hug before he eventually climbed in beside me.

Later, at a safe distance, I began considering the very different ways Dad and I had responded to that stressful situation we had found ourselves in, and it made me appreciate more deeply his gift for always choosing to take the time to love the person he is speaking to. Sometimes in this work we can get so caught up in measuring results and improving methodologies that we risk forgetting the person right in front of us: the person who is the reason for our work. We can do that too easily. It is not only dramatic situations and the fear of exploding shells that have led me to make that mistake. Much more often I have missed opportunities to listen to my co-workers or make friends with people in the communities we serve because I have been distracted by much more mundane things – perhaps the deadline for a report, the preparation of a presentation or a new fundraising idea bouncing about in my head. And meanwhile I have missed the chance of something much more important – the chance to build a relationship. Because, unless we do that, we cannot sincerely call this a work of love.

The human heart is no small thing. It can contain a love so vast it can overwhelm you and make you realise how very small you are. But sometimes our hearts – mine certainly – are not strong enough, not yet big enough. We need to find ways to exercise them and we need to learn from those who know how to love more deeply and more freely. For those reasons I am profoundly grateful for having had so many encounters with the human heart, in a multitude of places, while serving the mission of Mary's Meals.

Barunka lives in the Czech Republic. When she was three years old she was diagnosed with cancer. Today, at thirteen years old, she is very ill and a brain tumour has caused her to become completely blind. Her family is not rich and her treatments are financially demanding. In her newly dark world Barunka decided to begin helping hungry children by making bead bracelets and angels to raise funds for Mary's Meals. In this way she sends us regular donations. Barunka doesn't know what the future holds, but meanwhile she says that helping those children in faraway places makes her feel worthwhile. Recently she sent a number of us in Mary's Meals one of her lovely angels, along with a photograph of herself wearing a Mary's Meals T-shirt and a lovely smile. I carry it with me now. I wish she could see for herself how happy she looks, and I hope she knows how happy she makes so many of us.

Dear Mary's Meals

Enclosed is $55 to help feed another child. This comes from a man in a nursing home; he is wheelchair-bound, right-side paralysed and unable to speak. He is financially supported by Medicare and Medicaid; the $55 represents his entire savings. He pulled it out from different places after hearing about Mary's Meals. I am certain it will be put to good use.

With best wishes
A carer in the USA

On one occasion I had been invited to give a presentation at a gathering taking place at Edinburgh University. I had finished my little talk and was a few minutes into a question-and-answer session when someone's hand went up near the back row of the tiered lecture hall. I was feeling tired and a little daunted by the number of academics in the audience. As the microphone was brought to the person with their arm in the air, I was really hoping it wasn't going to be a difficult question. But it was.

'There are lots of people suffering terrible poverty in the UK. Just a few streets away from us there are kids living in a way you wouldn't believe – kids who are hungry. So why do you think we should be helping those children you are talking about, thousands of miles away, in the developing world?'

I paused for a moment as I raced through the file in my mind labelled: 'Answers to: Charity Begins at Home Questions'. I was about to select the answer called 'Statistics to Demonstrate that Poverty is far more Acute in the Developing World and on a Different Scale,' when I found myself saying something completely different.

'Because we have it in our hearts,' I said, realising as I did so that it didn't seem quite so profound when I said it, and so I continued by telling the story of how I came upon the answer in Malawi.

Perhaps to answer that question with a story was a bit of a cop-out. But I am aware of the limitations of trying to answer questions about the why of charity in any other way. We can of course provide plenty of evidence of need (and compare needs in answer to the specific question voiced that day in Edinburgh), and we can certainly present a sound logical case as to how, by helping the poorest and most vulnerable in our world, we will all ultimately benefit, but none of that will fully answer questions about the motives of our charity. Charity is love. It is difficult to prove the necessity of love at a particular moment – in fact it is impossible. The choice to love cannot be something obligatory – it needs to be freely chosen. And sometimes that choice will be absurd – beyond the limits of logic. And statistics aren't much use because love cannot be measured (demonstrated, yes, but not quantified).

This is one of the reasons why the heart can become an undervalued thing as a charitable organisation grows and develops in ways that sometimes need to mimic corporate organisations. At board meetings, in reports and during strategic discussions, all sorts of helpful data will be presented: financial information; statistics relating to donation trends; numbers of children fed; along with facts about certain activities that have been accomplished and certain opportunities that have presented themselves. It is hard to talk about matters of the heart in such an environment; difficult to do a check-up on the health of the beating heart when the one we are talking about isn't a physical pumping muscle like the one that a cardiologist can listen to and watch on a graph. We need to find ways to keep the heart at the centre of the conversation lest it be forgotten, and certainly the telling of true stories is one way to do that.

Storytelling is also a way to introduce people that need help to those who can provide it – even if they live on the other side of the world. The stories make it personal. They allow people to sit for a while in the warm dust of an African playground and get to know the child they fed that day. This is where charity begins. When we stand beside the one in need and know them even a little, then we are free to choose whether to let those feelings in our heart lead us to act.

And within that stirring of our heart we also find the strength to keep going. After months and years on the journey, when we are tired, discouraged, tempted to believe we have already done as much as we can – we go back there, to the source. We need, at all costs, to keep those feelings and the ones we serve right at the very centre of our mission. Amid the daily work that swamps and stresses us and pulls us in all sorts of directions, we need to find a way back to this thing in our heart – this yearning to reach out our hand to the one in pain.

But then, with our heart beating, we need to employ our minds too. Because our heart, if left to its own devices, can become a tyrant.

Part Two (The Head)

One day I noticed a homeless man sitting against the wall of a busy street in Glasgow. He had a paper coffee cup in front of him and some people, ahead of me on the pavement, threw coins into it as they passed him. I had the idea that I should instead get him something to eat and I turned back to a nearby bakery to buy him a pie and a flapjack. Feeling rather pleased with myself, and with a little tingle of anticipation at the happiness I was about to cause, I squatted beside the man and offered him the goodies.

'F*** off,' he said, with a scornful wave of his arm.

'I hate that sh**.'

His anger shocked me. I noticed a couple of people were staring at us. I felt humiliated and hurried on my way. And because I wasn't brave enough to continue the conversation, I never did learn anything more about that man's situation. Why was he so offended by me? Why was he in that situation in the first place? Would he have reacted that way to any offering of food or did he just hate Scotch pies?

Of course, there is a chance that he was just so angry at the whole world that he would have shouted and sworn at anyone who tried to engage with him. Maybe he wanted people to engage only with his paper cup and leave it at that. Maybe he was suffering from a mental illness. I don't know the answer to any of those things, nor do I pretend to have any expertise to offer on homelessness and how best to deal with it. I tell this story only to illustrate what can happen when our 'charitable acts' are motivated more by how we feel than by a genuine interest in the one we are 'helping'. We need to be willing to try to discover what would really help them most.

That is why genuine charity must employ the head as well as the heart. If we allow our decisions to be dictated entirely by our feelings, we should prepare ourselves for disaster – or at the very least public humiliation. Our emotions, if left to their own devices, are often a very poor guide in the practice of charity. While it is right and proper that we are first propelled towards charity by feelings of compassion, our first stop on the route to action should be the brain.

Let's suppose we happen upon someone who we recognise as being critically ill. Charity will want to enable them to receive professional medical care as quickly as possible. If, instead of using our phone to call for an ambulance, we choose to hold their hand and speak consoling words, because that makes us feel good or draws attention to ourselves, then we are certainly not practising charity – even though it might look as if we are. (Of course, holding their hand and consoling them might be a very good and extremely important charitable thing to do – but only after we have called for the ambulance.)

I am using an extreme example to make the point, but this choice – to pander to our own feelings, even when our head tells us that another course of action would better serve the person in need – is one that can happen in many different and sometimes subtle ways. And it can prevent us, as individuals or as organisations, from making any real progress in the pursuit of charity.

While charity that allows the head to dominate and becomes embarrassed by the heart can become cold, disrespectful and unable to appreciate the whole human being, charity that fails to give the head its place takes a very different wrong turning, but one that just as drastically takes us off course, leading us into a never-ending loop of sentimentality and self-gratification.

Genuine charity should indeed improve the lives of those who practise it faithfully, making them feel better as they become more fully human. But, paradoxically, the gifts they receive – such as deeper peace and joy – are fruits that are received by those who are not seeking them first and foremost. In fact, the most authentic practitioners of charity are not actually seeking anything at all except to love and serve the one in need.

Most of us, if we are willing to face the truth for any length of time, know that that kind of consistent purity is far from our current reach and something we can only aspire to. I am sure we all have moments in our life when we have done good things with completely selfless motives; to capture them and make them our way of life – that is a lofty goal indeed. But a wonderful one, perhaps the best a person could have and something we should never give up on, even when it feels impossible. But to make any progress towards it requires regular doses of the truth.

The cantankerous man on the pavement that day offered me a hard-to-swallow dollop of truth. He helped me to understand that I had been motivated by doing something that felt good to me at that moment, rather than taking the time to find out about what might be best for him.

If our desire is to help the suffering person as well as we possibly can, we need to *think* about it and often we need to allow our head to rule our heart. Informal 'charity of the heart', carried out by us as individuals, entirely in our control, or carried out with a group of friends, is something that usually feels great initially. However, even though a good work may be of very noble birth – rooted in the purist of motives and the doing of genuinely heroic deeds – it can also, quite easily, start to become self-serving as it goes on, creating a little kingdom, a certain status or a well-protected comfort zone which we can use to justify various superiority complexes.

The story of the development of Mary's Meals was punctuated by a series of decisions that allowed the head to rule the heart. Let me list just three such choices, early in our evolution:

1. We began this work by driving little truck-loads of aid to Medjugorje, a place of pilgrimage in Bosnia–Herzegovina; a place which we knew well long before

the war and one which – because of the vital part it played in our spiritual journey – held a deep emotional and spiritual attachment for us. It was a village that we loved and where we had friends. However, many other people from all over the world were also bringing aid to Medjugorje for the same reasons. And it certainly wasn't a crazy thing to be doing, given it was a well-located, secure base from which to distribute aid. However, as we began to think about it and look at the information, we realised that there were areas of huge need that were not attracting so much international aid and so in time we decided to serve them instead, taking unfamiliar roads, that led nowhere near Medjugorje, to unfamiliar places.

2. After progressing from small trucks to medium-sized trucks to enormous articulated lorries in order to keep up with the ever-increasing quantities of aid donations, and having developed a system to take commercial loads back from Eastern Europe to the UK to help finance the expensive transport costs, we began to look at the fact that there were commercial hauliers looking for payloads to take in the other direction. In time we decided it would be more cost-effective to pay them to deliver the aid to our by now well-established partner organisations in the former Yugoslavia. So we sold our trucks and gave up on our journeys across Europe and our regular visits to communities we had befriended.

3. There came a point when the ending of the terrible wars in Croatia, Bosnia–Herzegovina and Kosovo

coincided with new developments in our own work (which saw us funding projects such as children's homes in Romania) and we decided to phase out the collection and delivery of material aid. We could see that this was no longer the most appropriate way to help. This was no small change to accept for many people, who had become involved in a mission that had been born to help in that particular way and who for several years had devoted large chunks of their lives to the work of collecting, categorising, packaging and loading trucks. In our warehouses lasting friendships had been formed and daily routines created. Much of that goodwill was transferred to activities that supported our new approach, but assenting to the cessation of material aid deliveries required our heads to rule our hearts.

Listing these so briefly is to risk suggesting that these were easy decisions to make. They were not. They involved the kind of 'grief' we experience every time we let go of something we have become attached to. They were choices involving difficult discernment and the weighing of differing opinions. And the reality was that these stages of evolution involved making mistakes, changing our minds and causing good people to feel hurt.

To state that charity always needs to be rooted in, and informed by, truth seems like a thing so obvious it barely needs saying, but like many important things, practising it is much harder than preaching it. The truth can make dreadful demands of us. To learn that the years of hard work which have cost us so much have not been as effective as we thought, and that our way of working needs to be radically changed or dropped completely, could be a deeply traumatic event in our lives. When we proclaim happily that we want to be redundant one day (because that will mean the need we are addressing no longer exists), we might be speaking honestly, but when faced with that imminent reality, we might feel as if our sense of self-worth and identity are being ripped from us.

The denial of the truth also played a huge part in the scandal created by the depraved behaviour of those individuals working in Haiti after the earthquake. A lack of willingness to confront and tell the truth was what turned that event into a public scandal. Yes, the crimes committed were the real evil and cause, but if the response to these by the organisations involved had been different, then their reputations, and that of charities in general, would not have been so seriously damaged. I do sympathise with the organisations involved. For many years they had been carrying out great work, and continue to do so, all the while building up a reputation of credibility and trust. For them, and for all of us dependent on the goodwill of our supporters, trust is the most precious of commodities and the thought of losing it is a terrifying one.

On discovering that something has gone badly wrong within any organisation, the last thing we want to do is tell other people about it. If an individual has breached rules and dearly held values and the incident has been dealt with and learnt from through internal processes, it is easy to convince ourselves there is no need to let anyone else know. And sometimes, depending on the nature of the misdemeanour, its seriousness and whether failing to report it puts others at risk, that might even be the right decision. When weighing up whether to go public with bad news, the drastic impact that negative publicity could have will loom large – a loss of reputation, a decrease in funding, a queue of sick patients but no medicine to dispense. Add to that the fact that some sections of the media hold a negative position on certain types of charity and are looking for opportunities to support their views, and you can at least understand why some wrong decisions about transparency are made in these situations. But ultimately, parting company with the truth, no matter how uncomfortable the truth might be, never works out well in the long run.

At a personal level, in order to cope with the exacting and uncompromising nature of truth, we need to develop a certain detachment towards the things that make us feel good while practising charity. While learning to recognise and cherish the healthy long-term fruits of peace and joy that might come to us through our faithful involvement in a good cause, we should also find a way to ensure these don't depend on the success of our latest project, our role within it or any kind of recognition. We must strive for a certain hard-to-attain freedom in these things.

Another reason for not allowing our hearts sole responsibility in our decision-making is that our feelings, by their very nature, are fickle things. The zeal that led us to promise help to an organisation or person over a period of time might one day evaporate. We may get tired or perhaps feel distracted from our commitment by some other more interesting activity. That is when we need our minds to tell us loudly and clearly: 'It really doesn't matter how you *feel* this morning! What matters is your promise!'

That is when we need to get up and start cooking the porridge even though we might feel hungry ourselves; that is when we need to drag ourselves out there on another wet winter's day and begin shaking our collecting tin; that is when we need to stop prevaricating and phone our rather awkward neighbour and ask if they will lend a hand at the coffee morning. To do those unglamorous things when we do not feel like doing them – these are, perhaps, the most admirable acts of charity we can perform. They hold more worth than those first spontaneous things, carried out when our hearts are so full of compassion we could walk through walls in furtherance of our mission. No, our hearts cannot be trusted on their own with such mundane but crucial matters. We need to exercise our intellect and our will if we are serious about our pursuit of charity.

The truth has no wish to denigrate the heart. If it did so, it would no longer be the truth, for it has no sound reason to do so. When we let our heads rule our hearts while making decisions in the early days of our mission, some other interesting choices were made in addition to the three I listed – ones whose purpose was to honour and make more visible the crucial place of the heart. So, while we decided to stop delivering aid to Medjugorje, we chose to recognise the preciousness of that place within the Mary's Meals family (now dispersed across many countries around the world) by holding some of our global gatherings and meetings there and eventually creating a permanent organisational presence there. And in Scotland, having outgrown the tiny old shed which had become my office (after borrowing it from my father for the first collection of aid), and having built a new space for our growing team next door, we decided, instead of knocking it down, to keep that shed as our 'global HQ'. It remains today my office, in which I am writing this, and is a reminder to us of a few things, including our simplicity, our promise to our donors and our low-cost approach. It is also a reminder that within our work the heart – that is love – will never be left behind.

When we find a way for these things to work in harmony within us – and within charitable organisations – things more beautiful than we could ever imagine can start to happen.

We didn't know his name and he had no way of telling us. He looked about nine years old, dressed in a scruffy T-shirt and shorts. The police in Monrovia had found him two days earlier wandering alone in the city and put him in prison for the night. The next day, having heard something on the radio about our new school for the deaf, they drove out to Tubmanburg to find us and then left the voiceless child in our care. How could we have said no? We had already exceeded the maximum number of children we planned to enrol, but that figure had already had to be adjusted upwards more than once anyway, and the number of children we now thought we could accommodate and teach had reached sixty. Even as we walked Joseph (the name we had just given the silent boy) over to meet his new friends and join his first sign-language class, the carpenters could be heard urgently hammering and sawing the wood for extra bunk beds in the dormitories.

Our team had been encountering many deaf children in the villages of Liberia during and after a war that had deprived many of the most basic healthcare – healthcare which would

GIVE

have prevented things like ear infections causing their permanent loss of hearing. None had had the chance to learn sign language, and most had been shunned and cast to the very edges of their communities. I had met some of them during many visits to little villages nestled in the forests of Bomi County and Cape Mount.

A remarkable Dutch missionary called Liesbeth, who had already been working with deaf children among the Liberian refugee camps in neighbouring Ghana and had recently returned with co-workers who could teach sign language, began nagging me about the idea of a school for the deaf. This was just as we were beginning to concentrate on our new, all-consuming, mission of Mary's Meals and as we set up our first school feeding programmes here. I had also been busy explaining to everyone that we were now going to focus on this one crucial intervention only and not be distracted by other potential projects. But Liesbeth never gave up and nor did the children.

Thanks to them the Oscar Romero School for the Deaf was eventually born. A few years after its inauguration, while making another visit to our base in Tubmanburg, I attended a Sunday Mass. As usual I was struck by the gracefulness of the little liturgical dancers adorned in wonderful matching dresses, who danced up the aisle ahead of Father Garry and around the altar at certain points of the liturgy – a tradition I had often enjoyed here, and one taken very seriously by the children chosen to dance. Many long hours of practice are required before being able to participate in the Mass in such a perfectly choreographed and beautiful way.

But on that particular morning I was especially moved, for

100

this group of dancers were from the Oscar Romero school. The smiling children, who had once been shunned and rejected, were now in the centre of their community as it worshipped. And when it came to the Scripture reading one of their number, Esther, stood up confidently and signed to the church while someone else read the passage aloud. It was from the first chapter of the Gospel of Luke, where Mary the mother of Jesus praises God in the Magnificat. 'He has cast the mighty from their thrones and raised the lowly,' proclaimed Esther with her nimble hands.

Thankfully for those children, the head allowed the heart to win the argument on more than one occasion during the story of the Oscar Romero School for the Deaf. It could certainly be argued that this was foolish. The running of this school has sucked in enormous amounts of time and energy. The care of children with special needs has demanded a level of expertise we have often struggled to provide. The challenge of helping the young people to make the transition from the residential school to an independent life has been hugely difficult. Perhaps, it could be argued, that if we had not been distracted by this school and the responsibilities of running it and focused solely on our school feeding programme, we would be helping even more children across Liberia with those desperately needed daily school meals.

Maybe if we had understood more fully in advance the enormity of the challenge and the weight of the responsibilities, we would have resisted the urgent tugging of our heartstrings by those little ones in the villages. Or maybe, if we could have envisaged then that one Sunday morning, one of those rejected children would stand up and speak God's word to a packed church, we would have succumbed even more quickly.

Some of these questions have no right or wrong answer – they are simply choices we make along the way as best we can. And if all of us making such choices based them on identical criteria and evaluation of the same available data, we would all end up doing exactly the same things, thus leaving huge swathes of humanity abandoned and particular types of need completely unmet. Thank God for the different callings we as individuals and organisations seem to feel and the unique nature of each charitable mission. Perhaps even beyond the urging of our heart and the rationale of our head, there is something else at play which can prompt us towards a particular cry of need? The woman who sat down beside the homeless man in New York had carried out no research and positioned herself there with no intention of helping him change his life around. My little first effort in Bosnia was not the product of any analysis and it came with no plan beyond that one delivery of some gifts.

For those of us guided by our faith in a loving God we might call this other 'thing' the prompting of the Holy Spirit or God's providence or an answer to prayer. Others might talk about fate. Or, more simply, we can just think about the fact that when we find ourselves faced with someone in need and we have the ability to help them, then we should do so – without any previous plan, the need for analysis or a convoluted thought process. This must certainly be a valid approach for us as individuals, but maybe it can be even for organisations sometimes. It is a very big risk indeed to ignore the cry of the one in front of us, or the phone call from a co-worker in India whose village in Kerala has just been washed away by a flood and who is asking for support in helping the survivors, or a plea from a Muslim friend in Malawi to join with them in an effort to help the millions of starving people in Somalia because they have found a very effective way to do just that.

Plans have their place – an important one. But just as the heart can become a tyrant if not guided by the head, so too can the head, if it begins to ignore the heart by holding up a plan as our sole guide. We need to be very careful not to end up serving a plan rather than the people who need our help.

And so, for charity to be authentic and fruitful, the head and the heart have to work together in harmony and mutual respect. And that is what they wish to do. They are not sworn enemies. They do not fundamentally contradict each other. They need each other and contain each other. Any true intelligence cannot overlook the centrality of love and any authentic love cannot but wish to intelligently serve the one in need. Because that is the only way to serve them well.

On our journey so far, in order to pursue authentic charity, we have encountered some examples of charity gone wrong, including things that are no longer charity, and perhaps never were, but have assumed its title and its prestige. But I would like to point out that my overriding experience of working for . charity all these years has been one of being repeatedly humbled by people's goodness, humility and selflessness. A great international army, whose soldiers relentlessly and fear-lessly practise exquisite acts of charity, long ago conquered my heart. They are my guide and my inspiration.

My biggest fear in writing this book (and there are many,

given that I am daring to write about something I have not nearly mastered or even fully understood) is that I should inadvertently discourage anyone from carrying out even a single act of charity that they would otherwise have completed. These considerations about heart and head – please be careful not to let them delay your acts of goodness. Please do not begin agonising over the purity of your motives while the person in front of you – or even on a YouTube video of a faraway land – experiences a suffering that you could help relieve. Maybe consistent purity of motive in the practice of charity is as far from your grasp as it is from mine, but if we aspire to its attainment we can only journey towards it by trying and sometimes failing. And if anyone tells you they knew what they were doing at the start of such a journey, and where it would lead them, they themselves long ago parted company with the truth.

5

Charity and Beyond

'Go back?' he thought. 'No good at all! Go sideways?
Impossible! Go forward? Only thing to do! On we go!'
So up he got and trotted along with his little sword
held in front of him and one hand feeling the wall,
and his heart all of a patter and a pitter.

J. R. R. TOLKIEN, *THE HOBBIT*

The journey, beyond a first little act of charity, can lead us along many paths which may look and feel radically different from each other and from that original good deed. Charity draws us, first of all, to the immediate need of the person in front of us. It leads us to meet that need as best we can; a hot meal for a homeless man, medical aid for the earthquake victim or food for the one ravished by hunger. But soon love desires other things for the one who endures such deprivations. We would like that person to be rehabilitated and once again live a dignified life, no longer reliant on charity. We want to prevent that person – and others – from ever finding themselves in such dire need again. If the environment in which the person lives is one of crippling poverty, we will wish for them – and their community – to escape that and will strive to help their society develop economically and in other ways. Thus, we may embark on activities in support of international or human development. We may also recognise that the person is oppressed, perhaps even denied their basic human rights, and robbed of any opportunity to escape the situation in which they suffer. We may feel compelled to join a struggle for justice. We may feel moved by the plight of the planet, our common home, and become engaged in efforts to address climate change and environmental degradation. We might form the view that things will only change fundamentally if the political situation is altered, and so devote ourselves to a political cause or movement. And then we may seek to prevent such political situations ever recurring, or to work to eliminate poverty and the need for charity altogether by embracing and promoting a particular ideology.

So along the way charity begins to take different forms and exercise various roles – and may even be left behind altogether. And when that happens, sometimes those who abandon charity begin to disdain her, portraying her as naïve, old-fashioned, hypocritical, self-serving and a hindrance to the more important work of development.

Mohammed Yunus, the globally renowned 'banker of the poor', pioneer of microcredit and microfinance initiatives, founder of the Grameen Bank and winner of the Nobel Peace Prize, once wrote:

When we want to help the poor, we usually offer them charity. Most often we use charity to avoid recognizing the problem and finding the solution for it. Charity becomes a way to shrug off our responsibility. But charity is no solution to poverty. Charity only perpetuates poverty by taking the initiative away from the poor. Charity allows us to go ahead with our own lives without worrying about the lives of the poor. Charity appeases our consciences.

Professor Yunus is someone who deserves respect and his achievements speak for themselves, but this particular quotation makes me a little sad that someone who has dedicated his life to helping the poor escape poverty would describe charity in this manner. Has he, tragically, managed to miss the authentic love that must abide amid the poor of his homeland, Bangladesh, as it does among people everywhere? I suppose he is talking primarily about international aid and I understand some of the sentiments he expresses, but his words lead me to wonder if he has only ever encountered the distorted types of charity that develop in the absence of truth rather than the real thing? Because authentic charity wants what he wants – the empowerment of the poor and the finding of solutions that will set them free. It is also interested in 'recognising the problem and finding the solution'. However, while charity does that, it does not make the mistake of focusing only on the cause and forgetting about the need. It cannot ever abandon the one suffering at this minute while it works on its solution for a better tomorrow. History offers us plenty of lessons about what happens when ideas and solutions become more important than people and the current reality of their lives. We cannot walk away from the woman yelling for help under the remains of her recently collapsed house in order to sit down in our offices and begin designing earth-quake-proof new homes. We cannot ignore the malnourished child with the empty bowl as we stride towards the fields of the farmer to engage in a project to improve crop yields.

Tired aphorisms about fishing rods rather than fish and 'hand ups' rather than handouts, while certainly containing some important truths when used in the right context, are repeated lazily and endlessly. Of course for many a fishing rod is better than a fish, but only if they have the strength to cast it and only if there are some fish left in the river. Otherwise one fish to eat would be of much greater value. And I would have thought there is merit in sometimes just holding the hand of a distraught person without trying to pull them in some upward direction of your choosing. But that is not to disagree with the sentiment – not at all. Charity must yearn to set the person free from whatever holds them in a place of suffering.

And, of course, charity, if we are not careful, can inadvertently hamper efforts towards human development. Charity that fails to see the poor themselves as the most important part of the solution is very likely to stifle healthy growth and development. Every opportunity must be taken to empower local communities. Ideally, they are the ones who initiate and lead projects aimed at improving their lives and the lives of their children. Those of us from outside will, hopefully, have only temporary roles, limited to 'filling some gaps' by providing crucial skills and resources that the community, at that moment, cannot otherwise access. Unfortunately, in the very poorest countries in the world those gaps can be enormous. Outside interventions, in order to be helpful and leave something sustainable behind, might require considerable time. But that doesn't mean we can lose sight of that ultimate goal; it simply means that sometimes, groups of people from different countries may need to walk together for some years in order to build something that will last; something that will turn the tide that has for centuries been flowing in a different direction.

This craving to see the poor set free from chronic poverty and dependence on aid is the same one that led our mission to evolve from the one driving aid to refugees in Bosnia to one that sets up community-owned school feeding programmes in places of education. While on that long journey we came face to face with a multitude of children who were missing school because of hunger and poverty. For them and their families, the pressing need to eat overwhelmed and snuffed out longer-term aspirations and ambitions. So instead of sitting looking at blackboards in classrooms, they were sifting through rubbish looking for things to sell, or helping their mother carry goods to market, or smashing rocks into gravel with a homemade hammer, or cutting sugar cane for the master who had bought them – or doing even more terrible things for the kind of people who buy children. All so that they and their families could eat. And meanwhile they missed school and the education that could have served as their only ladder out of poverty. Condemned to a life of poverty, they will one day be raising their own children in similar circumstances. And so it goes on: hunger through the generations; hunger acting as both the cause and the result of chronic poverty; chronic poverty acting as both the cause and the result of hunger.

We came to believe that something as simple as one daily meal in a place of education could help break this pernicious cycle. When local volunteers first began serving those meals, consisting of locally grown food, to the children of their school, very quickly we could see that it was working. Children who had never come to school before came because of the promise of a mug of porridge. Children who used to come just on some days came nearly every day. Children who were previously unable to concentrate and stay awake in class because of hunger were now able to concentrate and learn. On seeing this happen, we decided to focus entirely on this one intervention and to work relentlessly to enable as many as possible of the world's poorest children to benefit from it.

Today, Mary's Meals are served in many different countries in a huge variety of cultures and environments but always consisting of the same thing; one meal every day cooked and served by local volunteers, and always with the same result – the enabling of the poorest children to gain an education. The model is being continually refined and adapted to different settings, but we can see that this simple thing works.

The beauty of Mary's Meals is that in this little act of serving a meal, two of charity's greatest desires are fulfilled – the desire to meet the immediate need of the hungry child and the desire to set them free from poverty. Of course, unfortunately, it is not as straightforward as serving one meal and everyone living happily ever after. That meal is not a panacea for all forms of poverty. There are lots of other constraints and complexities in regard to the future of each child. But it can certainly be seen, in the lives of many young people who once ate Mary's Meals at school, that the gaining of an education, made possible by that meal, has indeed enabled them to win some epic battles with poverty.

I like very much that Mary's Meals is, simultaneously, an act of basic charity meeting an immediate need, while also being a deed aimed at tackling the underlying causes of poverty, because too often these two kinds of charity are portrayed as being mutually exclusive. They are not. To suggest otherwise is to create an unnecessary war like that which can occur between the heart and the head in the practice of charity.

I fully respect that in the pursuit of charity some individuals and organisations will move from one form of charity to another. This seems like a very reasonable journey and will take us on a well-travelled road. However, that should not lead us to despise a mission focused on simple acts of charity – to treat those simple acts as something naïve or contrary to the desire to support longer-term human development. Both these things, if authentic, are rooted in the same love for the person and desire for them to experience good things – now and in the future. It is true that the way in which we meet basic urgent needs can support or hinder efforts to set people and their communities free from poverty, and therefore must be considered very carefully. For example, within the context of Mary's Meals, we have a multitude of choices to make about the methodology of providing the meal and when making them, our goal of seeing the community we serve move away as soon as possible from dependency on our provision is a key factor. This is why, for example, we use locally produced food as much as possible. In this way we support the development of the local economy and the smallholder farmers. In addition, we are clear from the outset that each school community is responsible for the daily work of the project, such as the recruitment and management of volunteer cooks. Our role is mainly the provision of the food, and the programme is deliberately designed in a way that is conducive to our withdrawal on the happy day that the food can be provided by the country's government or some other local enterprise.

Simple, immediate charity, if carried out thoughtfully, is not an enemy of development; rather, it can be the first essential foundation stone. To suggest that it is a foe would be to lose sight of the fact that each has the same beginning and end: the suffering person it seeks to serve – because charity doesn't serve ideas or solutions, it serves people. But things aren't always black and white.

On one occasion an organisation running schools in Haiti approached us to ask if we might be willing to provide meals to their pupils. In principle we were. We had been working in Haiti for some years and recognised the enormous need for school feeding programmes; many children were not enrolled in school and many more who were in class were too hungry to learn. And we were already providing tens of thousands of children with school meals in other parts of the country. However, one of our great challenges there was that we were unable to access affordable, reliable sources of locally grown ingredients, given that Haiti, as a whole, was producing much less food than its population required. This meant that most of the meals we were providing there consisted of imported food. As our discussions with the group running those schools continued, this became an insurmountable stumbling block. They had an admirable philosophy about projects being sustainable and the idea of using imported food bothered them greatly (as it did us) and they, therefore, politely declined our offer of providing free meals. We reiterated our own position, which was a very strong preference to use locally produced food – as we were doing in most other countries where we worked – and that we would continue working towards achieving that in Haiti. But meanwhile, the only way in which we could provide meals to pupils in Haiti reliably and at any scale was to use food grown in other countries. We never did begin serving meals in those schools, and when I checked several years later no one else had either. And so the children in those communities remained hungry.

Through the conversations we had with the group running the schools I came to like them and respect them. They were doing amazing things for the children of that area by setting up schools. I admired, too, their determination to stick to their principles and their willingness to say 'no thanks' to a significant offer of help because it seemed contrary to their philosophy. But those children continued to experience a hunger that no child in this world should ever suffer, and the needs of a child today should never be sacrificed to some 'god of sustainability'. Yes, let's strive with all our might to set communities free from poverty. Yes, a huge priority for Haiti is for it to find a way to produce more food. And yes, ideally, the meals we serve are locally grown (and even in the years since this incident we've made good progress in being able to do that more often in Haiti). But no, the needs of a child today cannot be subjugated to a future we can never be certain of. And how strange to think that the health and education of a child plays a less important part in creating a truly sustainable future for Haiti than the buying of local crops. If the child cannot live and grow, conversations about sustainability are superfluous – as are more general conversations about the future.

I do not question that that group in Haiti loved those children sincerely. They had already amply demonstrated that by their actions. Perhaps these conflicting opinions can arise through the adherence to different priorities, or through being unclear about the order of those. For example, if engaged in running school feeding programmes it is essential to be clear on whether the primary objective is the efficient reliable serving of a daily meal or the support of local agriculture. When we are unclear on our hierarchy of priorities we risk falling into the trap of trying to solve everything at once and failing in all of it.

Sustainability is a word used often and in a variety of ways during conversations about development. Many charitable missions have failed the probing of a potential grant-making donor on the criterion of sustainability. The word is often raised as a question when such funding bodies and others working in international development encounter missions, including Mary's Meals, which engage in the provision of something as basic as food. The very notion conjures up thoughts of old-fashioned, naïve charity uninterested in, or obstructive to, international development. These kinds of grant funders are extremely exercised by exit strategies within particular timeframes of their choosing – often three or five years.

Anyone who has seen the debris left behind by well-meaning but silly projects in the developing world will understand why a potential funder would want to talk about an exit strategy and long-term sustainability. Rusting water pumps that no local person has the equipment to maintain are a classic case in point, as are all sorts of projects that flourished for a short time before running out of money and closing down, leaving nothing behind that continues to help anyone: a hulking, empty college building with no staff or students; an overgrown, abandoned row of weedy fish ponds; a freshly painted large nursery built, curiously, on top of a steep hill, lying still and empty while in the village below children learn outside under a tree.

Someone responsible for distributing government funding for international development or running a philanthropic foundation would not be doing their job properly if they failed to ask questions about future plans and transition to local ownership. And certainly it can be extremely important to think hard about what an exit strategy looks like for any project, and to ensure that this is incorporated into its initial design. This was something we failed to do well when we set up the beautiful school for the deaf children in Liberia, and our lack of planning has caused us many headaches in the time since as a result.

At the same time, I worry that many great projects have been strangled before birth because they were unable to articulate a convincing exit strategy at the outset – or because the exit strategy identified could not realistically take place within the funder's stipulated timeframe. It amazes me that we so often convince ourselves that centuries of underdevelopment and endemic abject poverty can be turned around and solved in three or five years, or that governments with budgets much smaller than those of many individual corporate organisations should somehow be able to find the means to fund new initiatives that don't, in the short term, provide them with any new revenue.

More than once, experts working for a donor government's international development agency suggested to us that we were causing an unwelcome problem by attracting extra children into government schools that were already short of teachers and classrooms. We told them that we were not creating the problem; rather, we were just making it much harder to ignore. Surely, we asked, they weren't suggesting that it would be a better option to leave those children out of sight and out of school? Surely we could not just abandon the very poorest little ones? It seemed from some of their responses that they were indeed suggesting just that. When, despite their lack of support, we continued to feed the 'problem' (the poorest children), and thus boosted school enrolment, sometimes the government would respond by building extra classrooms or adding some more teachers in line with their commitment to providing universal free primary school education for all. When this didn't happen, classes that already had ninety or 100 children became classes of perhaps 120 or 130 children – far from ideal but, frankly, I do not believe the already poor standard of education became any poorer. Meanwhile many thousands of children who had previously not set foot in a classroom began to learn to read and write at least.

Another potential funder that was active in Malawi in the early years of our work was the large foundation of a wealthy entrepreneur. They too repeatedly shunned our efforts to seek their support, telling us that they didn't believe our model was sustainable. At that time we were serving perhaps 100,000 children each school day in that country and wished to expand to other communities that were waiting. A few years later, during the global financial crash, the entrepreneur and his foundation suffered catastrophic financial losses. They suddenly had to withdraw support from some of the projects they supported. Someone I knew who had moved his family to Africa in order to work on one of them was suddenly without a job and home – but he was the first to acknowledge that this was only a minor inconvenience compared to the hardship that it had caused local families who were dependent on those projects.

That, and other experiences, have led me to distrust some of the talk about sustainability. We should be very careful about who and what we put our faith in when it comes to certain matters relating to the future. This is one of the reasons we have chosen, primarily, to build our mission on a grassroots movement, consisting of a vast multitude of 'little acts of love' carried out each day by countless people in different countries, believing this to be a much more reliable source of income than a small number of large grants dictated by funding cycles or the financial performance of an individual business or the often-changing policies of a government department. And this funding model provides us with another crucial advantage – it leaves us free to make decisions about the length of our intervention. This is important because the provision of school meals to the very poorest communities is about generational change rather than short-term goals and exit strategies (although every serving of a meal to a hungry child also has a very immediate and dramatic impact). One day we wish to see the government of Malawi run their own school feeding programme without any need of outside help, but their tiny budget and national economy mean that cannot happen soon. We work with them and encourage them to take steps towards it, while being willing to walk with the communities for however long it takes for us to become redundant, believing that those little ones eating and learning today will be the ones who will tomorrow start and grow businesses, improve their country's agriculture, elect good governments and win the enormous battles their nation faces. They, not we, are the ones to fight those battles and, armed with health and at least a basic education, please God they will win them. But when and how exactly we don't pretend to know.

This willingness to accompany those communities over long periods of time is not to ignore the risk of creating a dependency culture, although that is another one of those phrases repeated too readily and sometimes unhelpfully. Are there any children in this world who are not dependent on others for their daily food? And never mind children, are any of us truly independent of others when it comes to our basic needs being met? Of course not. The question is really about who we are dependent on and why. And the plates of beans being devoured by a group of children sitting in the shade of an old tree in their playground taste no different to them whether they are being paid for by a government, a foreign business man or an elderly lady in Belgium who makes a monthly donation.

It is clear, though, that those children, and their children after them, will be much more capable of making their own choices if they have learnt to read and write and have not had their physical and cognitive development permanently impaired by malnutrition. And their governments, too, will become more empowered as the population they serve becomes better educated and more productive. But these things take time. Probably longer than one generation. And that doesn't always allow grantmakers to tick their boxes or entrepreneur philanthropists to deliver their solutions or politicians to point to change that is dramatic enough to match their rhetoric.

The voicing of unrealistic timeframes and solutions was carried out loudly and irresponsibly after the earthquake in Haiti. Prominent foreign politicians expressed worthy sentiments about 'building back better' and in their bombast suggested they would very quickly solve the fundamental issues facing Haiti by sending in a few experts alongside the billions of dollars donated in response to the disaster. But instead of witnessing a wonderful economic transformation, even the most basic rehabilitation efforts became horribly bogged down. Six months after the earthquake I returned to Haiti and found Father Tom still sleeping in his one-man tent in the courtyard, despite the fact they had rebuilt some reasonable sleeping quarters beside their old house.

'Today there are still hundreds of thousands of Haitians living in pathetic tents. It's a scandal. And as long as they have to do that, so will I!' he answered when I asked him why.

The idealistic confidence that believes engrained national poverty can be solved quickly, based on some good ideas and short-term initiatives, can be tempting and exhilarating – and is often prompted by the best of motives. But it can do immense damage too. In the years since the earthquake many have held up the lack of real progress in Haiti as an example of aid not working. Those criticisms have often been valid, but the proclamation of those unrealistic expectations has certainly helped fuel feelings of disillusionment with the efforts. And again, perhaps a clearer differentiation between immediate humanitarian efforts and longer-term development initiatives would have helped.

Sometimes we should accept that we cannot immediately solve everything we would like to solve without letting that diminish our resolve to relieve the person suffering today. Nor should we see the fact that some change takes time – even generations – as a reason not to set out on the path. If at the outset we had prepared ourselves well for a long journey we might well have reached some amazing destinations by now, instead of turning back at the first onset of tired limbs and blistered feet.

I spent much of my youth climbing the hills around our home in Scotland with my father, a deer stalker. To begin with, like any small child, I would set off with a ridiculous burst of energy, running and scrambling up steep heathery slopes, wondering why Dad was walking so slowly. Inevitably, before very long I would be asking if we were nearly there and, when discovering we were not, asking if we could go home because my legs were aching and my lungs were bursting, while my dad marched inexorably upwards at the same pace he had adopted at the beginning. It was some time before I learnt to employ a 'stalker's pace', as he used to call it, and even longer until I began to find joy in the steady progress of a long day's hiking. That is sometimes a good way to approach works of charity and development. At times, in the pursuit of charity, we may not even be climbing towards a summit of any sort. The charity we practise may not have an end goal, an exit strategy or any success beyond the simple choice to journey together – at least not any we will see with our own eyes. The accompaniment of the terminally ill, the feeding of a child with special needs and the caring for the person suffering a mental illness – these are just some of the tasks that often do not involve some solution or wonderful transformation. These works of faithful love are not sustained and rewarded by progress towards any target, and are all the more noble for it. I wish there was a greater appetite for lacing our hiking boots, packing our provisions and preparing for all weathers, instead of rushing out of the door with a desire to be a record-breaking sprinter.

That a journey together needs to take longer is not always something to fear. Indeed, if the relationship with our fellow travellers is a happy one and we have remembered to pack our map and compass (or we have learnt well the art of navigating by the stars), then the journey itself can be a joy. The blessings of the modern age of communications are many. Not only do they allow us to become aware of the desperate needs of our brothers and sisters on another continent; they can allow us, in a certain sense, to walk with them, to befriend them and to be in community with them. And as long as those relation-ships are respectful and free, then the opportunities they pres-ent of global fraternity are surely a good thing for the human family?

When we do our sponsored run with hundreds of others, sweating through crackling autumn leaves, knowing that our co-workers in a distant country are breathing hard as they carry the food that our fundraising event will provide up a steep wooded path to their mountain village school, we might feel a very rare sense of oneness with those distant people. We simply want to see the hungry child fed that day – all of us – and despite the enormous disparities that divide us, in that task at least, we are one. And that is a very beautiful thing – something to be appreciated and exalted rather than denigrated as naïve.

Sometimes it might be proposed that this feeling flows in one direction only. It might be doubted that the barefoot community slogging up the path to their school with huge weights of food on their heads feel the same joy or the same connectedness to those running in the park in that faraway, unimaginably rich country. But that would be a mistake. You would know that their joy is very real if you had ever had the privilege of climbing those mountain paths with them, enveloped by their singing voices and laughter. This kind of work for the hungry child makes people happy everywhere. And as for the feeling of connectedness working in both directions? I do remember that once we were asking ourselves the same question in regard to the placing of signs on new school kitchens with the names of donors who had funded them. We knew that to see the photographs of these signs was a wonderful, tangible thing for those generous donors, but we wondered how they would be perceived by the impoverished communities whose children were served by these kitchens. But before we had a chance to go further in exploring that, we were contacted by our teams in those countries, saying that some of the communities whose kitchens did not have signs on their schools were complaining. They were asking why a neighbouring school was connected to a particular donor and they were not. They felt a little neglected, a little unloved.

We have in the years since then worked harder on ensuring that communications flow in both directions so that we are not just telling donors stories of the children who eat the meals, but we are also telling those communities about the donors – stories of their little acts of love and their lives. When done thoughtfully and sensitively, this is hugely important in building fraternity and mutual respect. And it can fundamentally change the attitudes of the communities receiving help when they learn how and why this support is arriving. To know that the meals your children are eating have been provided by individuals who are making personal gifts is to appreciate that something very different from the aid programmes provided by governments or faceless international organisations is happening. Telling each other our stories is a powerful way to build a global family as we journey on through the park or up the mountain.

And sooner or later on this journey, whether we are jogging in our fashionable training shoes or walking barefoot with 25 kilogrammes of corn on our heads, we will happen upon another signpost with the word 'Justice' on it.

6

Mapping the Stars

To reach a port we must set sail –
Sail, not tie at anchor.
Sail, not drift.

FRANKLIN D. ROOSEVELT

Among the many roadside stalls in chaotic Monrovia, towards the end of the hideous war in Liberia, were those known locally as 'Buy Your Own'. These were selling loot: all kinds of possessions stolen by the various armed factions, many of them comprising child soldiers, who terrorised and stripped the properties of Liberia like a machine-gun-toting plague of locusts. I saw many buildings laid bare, not just of the things that might obviously be looted, but even of electrical cables, tin roofing sheets, doorknobs – indeed the doors themselves. All kinds of stories circulated of people being stripped of their belongings at gunpoint – some gruesome, some funny. These street stalls very kindly gave you the opportunity to buy back your own belongings, if you were good at haggling and got there before someone else who coveted your possessions. The

Archbishop of Monrovia was late in his shopping expedition, allowing his distinctive hat and garments to be purchased by an infamous fighter who was subsequently sighted in battle wearing flowing purple vestments and a white mitre on his head. Meanwhile, my friend and co-worker Father Garry Jenkins was more successful in buying back his possessions, sending out Liberian accomplices to haggle for the books and Bibles that had once made up his precious little library.

The injustice we might witness when pursuing charity can sometimes look like those 'Buy Your Own' markets. Things that already belong to people are repositioned as something to be sold to them or given them in an act of 'charity'. The multi-national mining company which has greedily ravished Liberia of its minerals without respecting the basic dignity of those digging in the mud for its gold has been engaged in looting just as surely as the crazy guy with the machine gun dressed as a bishop. And when that successful company eventually builds a little village school in the name of their foundation and puts a sign on it for us all to see their benevolence, they are still looters. The things they offer back to the Liberian people in fact already belong to them.

And when people like me, who live in a country that has become wealthy, in no small part, through colonising and enslaving millions of people, ridicule the people of Haiti for their inability to escape chronic poverty, ignorant of, or choosing to forget that the people of that nation:

- were captured, enslaved and forced to work in plantations while wearing iron masks to prevent them from eating the sugar cane that was making their masters incredibly wealthy;
- were brutally prevented from forming any kind of family life;
- on average could expect to live for just seven years after they walked, emaciated, from the stinking bowels of the ship in which they had been chained for weeks as it ploughed through the Atlantic;
- incredibly, staged an uprising which, at great cost of life and against all the odds, overthrew the French Empire, breaking the fetters that had held them fast, and began building a new future in the land of their exile;
- then found themselves charged with crippling 'reparation payments' by their former French masters (aided and abetted by the British and Americans) in return for recognition of their independence, paying compensation for 'losses suffered' by the slave owners ('Buy Your Own' is not a new concept) equating to US$21 billion today, which took until 1947 to pay off, largely financed by felling and selling much of their precious native forest, leaving behind barren eroded hills on which it is increasingly hard to grow things,

we should instead shut up and hang our heads in shame.

I am not suggesting that all of us living in countries that once grew rich through empire building and the exploitation of other peoples should exist in a permanent state of guilt for the wrongs done by our ancestors. But perhaps at least an awareness of the injustices carried out to create such wealth in our lands and such scandalous inequality should make us slow to judge others for their own poverty. Even though we are not personally responsible, a certain sense of shame might be appropriate. And if any other motivation were needed to embark on works of charity and justice for the world's poorest nations, surely a basic knowledge of history can provide that in abundance.

When, while pursuing charity, we come across that sign-post marked 'Justice', we cannot ignore it. For it would be strange simply to keep giving gifts to a person who is being repeatedly robbed and left destitute without ever trying to do something to protect them from the robber. It would be perverse to keep putting plasters on the bleeding knees of the schoolchild without dealing with the playground bully. It would be peculiar to work to erect tents for displaced people while remaining uninterested in who is evicting them from their homes and why.

However, while we cannot ignore that sign, we are not all obliged to take that particular road. Those who do – and carry on down that path while remaining rooted in charity and truth – should be revered. They are like the knights of old, donning their armour and taking up a fearless fight on behalf of the poor, oppressed and voiceless. That particular way leads to political activism, to battles for civil rights – to revolution, even. It is a path previously trodden by some of the great heroes of the human race: Mahatma Gandhi, Martin Luther King and Nelson Mandela, to name but three. These are the figures we learn about and are inspired by in school. They are the ones who fought the good fight ferociously without losing their charity (or at least repenting and regaining it when they did), resisting the temptation to start wars in which some would win and some would lose, and instead striving for change that would bring about a better future for all. Their missions were not about the re-ordering of society so that those currently oppressed could take their turn at oppressing someone else; rather, their vision was of a better, more just life for everyone. They engaged in peculiar forms of combat such as non-violent protests and the leading of peaceful rebellions that overthrew tyranny and changed the world for ever – even while dissuading the victors from taking the revenge that could have been theirs.

The world needs more of these sorts of people; people who can harness all their righteous anger and stay true in the heat of battle. They are rare indeed, and the road to which that signpost takes us is a treacherous one. The fight for justice can make us more noble, or can distort and diminish us if we allow ourselves to hate the oppressor and eventually all who do not share our worldview. We can spend our lives focused on the 'bad guys' and forget ever to challenge ourselves. Politicians (as a general group) the world over tend to be unpopular for a reason. The lure of power is strong enough to pull many a good person from the path they intended to take, separating them too often from the truth and purity of their original intention. Too frequently it becomes about them and their party. Too easily they forget about the human person. Too often they end up serving a political idea rather than the suffering people on whose behalf they originally took up their struggle. The desire to win and succeed becomes all-consuming, even to the point when personal beliefs and convictions are abandoned in a race for popularity and votes. Truth itself can become a victim of the murderous wiles of public image considerations. And yet the role of politicians and governments should be entirely about justice and upholding it.

I write these things not to discourage good people from becoming involved in politics or leading civil action in pursuit of justice. More than ever we need good people to devote their lives to these things. I list the pitfalls only to try to demonstrate why activities which focus on the fight for justice, if they are to remain true and noble, must stay rooted, always, in charity and truth. And to stay rooted when treading that road is an enormously difficult thing to do, requiring a very strong moral compass, abundant self-knowledge, humility, and probably exceptional stubbornness too.

While I am not sure that the vital works involved in that particular path (politics, advocacy, civil rights activism) should still be called charity, they most certainly should still be informed and motivated by it. The same love for the suffering person and the same desire that they, and all in society, might attain a better, more fully human, life, must continue to burn brightly in the heart of those engaged in such tasks, as should a passion for the truth. For if we remain devoted to charity and truth when we choose to work in these other fields related to justice and human development, we will know that these things existed long before us. Truth transcends us and our particular mission. We cannot create it in our own image and likeness. At best we can only be its servant, among a multitude of other good servants, today and through the ages. We are not the inventors of truth or charity. Heaven help us if we ever start to believe we are.

And in the same way that it would be absurd for those involved in certain types of international development work to despise works of charity that are aimed simply at meeting the basic needs of people today, so it would be a mistake for those who take up the fight for justice to think this supersedes charity. Charity cannot replace justice. But justice does not make charity obsolete.

Madagascar, March 2019

In the stark dormitories where the youngsters sleep two to a bed on wooden bunks with no mattresses, I notice a small hole has been smashed in the plasterboard ceiling. One of the younger children apparently tried to escape through the roof last week. His desperate attempt was futile.

In the prisons of Madagascar hundreds of children as young as nine years old are incarcerated. Many of them were living on the streets and are alleged to have been involved in petty crime before being imprisoned – around 80 per cent of them are still awaiting trial. Some young French volunteers working as lay missionaries in Madagascar discovered this population of children when they began visiting prisons here. In 2014 it led them to found a new organisation, Grandir Dignement, with the purpose of helping this population of vulnerable children. Among their activities was the setting up of educational opportunities – including training in brick-laying and agriculture – to arm the youngsters with skills that could provide some hope on their release. But it soon became apparent that the lack of consistent provision of food in the prisons and the resultant hunger, ill health and anxiety among the 'students' undermined any meaningful attempts to learn. That is when Grandir Dignement approached us, explaining the situation and asking if we might provide daily meals in the prison. In the time since we began doing that, the impressive team at Grandir Dignement have been able to concentrate on their skills training courses and also their strong focus on defending the rights of these children in law. They accompany the children from the time of their arrests and look for alternatives to imprisonment, while working with the government to try to change the current way of doing things and bring about an end to the incarceration of children. Their fight for justice on behalf of these children is an impassioned and fierce one. Please God, their efforts will soon mean there are no children to feed in such detention centres in Madagascar, but while there are, our simple work of charity in providing a daily meal enables the impressive team at Grandir Dignement to focus on the more demanding work of seeing justice done for each child, and changing the systems and attitudes that currently result in their imprisonment. This fight for justice is being built upon the most basic act of charity (the provision of food), which in this case is seen as a key foundation stone rather than something obsolete when the struggle moves on towards the pursuit of justice and systemic change.

But, noble though justice is, charity remains even greater, because it not only desires that the person is given what belongs to them (and it should wish for that first) – it wants to give even more. It wants to give gratuitously, unnecessarily, unobligated by rights or duties. Justice, if it was in charge of one of those 'Buy Your Own' markets on the sorry streets of Monrovia, would ensure that the war-weary shopper regained all their own belongings without any charge. If charity was running the stall, it would do the same, but then it might also hand the customer a gift – say, a bunch of fresh bananas and a packet of sweet biscuits – because it noticed the person's hunger. And then, seeing how weak they look, it might offer to help carry their possessions and their gifts home for them. And on the way it will talk to them about their life, because it sees their loneliness and sadness and desire for human company.

Justice is essential. Charity is that and more.

A sense of justice will also leave us unable to ignore the groaning of our planet. Our home, the Earth, seems to be in great pain; perhaps even in crisis. As participants in a society of rampant consumerism, we, the wealthy of the world, are the primary cause of this degradation of the planet and the suffering it is already causing some of the world's poorest people. If we have a passion for justice and a love for the poorest of the poor, we will not be able to see the pressing environmental issues of our day as something we have no personal obligation towards. Those of us whose charity is focused on the human person cannot view such matters as something unconnected to humanity, but rather we must realise, urgently, that the human person's house is becoming uninhabitable. And we must know that we human beings are connected in all sorts of ways to every aspect of creation, and our personal responsibilities in this area must eventually affect our daily choices. If our response to this situation is rooted in justice, it cannot be confined to telling countries who remain in poverty, but are still blessed with rainforests and other natural resources, to do what we never did in the history of our developed nations and simply refrain from benefiting from them while their people go hungry. That is not a voice of justice; it is the sound of rank hypocrisy. Long ago we exploited our own resources – our coal, our oil reserves, our forests, our lakes and the sea off our coasts – and became richer than any societies before us. We have created lifestyles and ways of living that are unsustainable. If similar lifestyles were to be enjoyed by the majority of our brothers and sisters on the planet, the current crises would soon become catastrophic. It clearly is not possible for everyone on the planet to consume as voraciously as we do. We should remember that as we engage with our brothers and sisters in the developing world and recognise that ours is not the high moral ground, and that the ground that they till and plant and live upon belongs to them more than it belongs to us.

On one memorable occasion, when visiting a primary school in the Eastern Province of Zambia, we encountered a large bull elephant. Thankfully, he had turned up his long nose at the delicious porridge being served to the children and was instead browsing the spiky leaves from the top of a tree a few hundred metres from the school gates. On the gable end of the main classroom block the children had painted a fascinating mural which depicted the struggle of their community, who, for as long as anyone could remember, had been hunters. A series of images, beginning with men hiding behind rocks with bows and arrows and ending with people in four-wheel-drive vehicles holding binoculars, told an interesting story. Things have been changing rapidly here in an area dominated by enormous, world-renowned national parks. The new tourism and conservation projects are bringing some welcome opportunities, but they are also bringing hardships and some local anger in this terribly impoverished part of the world. 'It seems there is now more value placed on the life of one elephant than on the future of our children,' a local leader complained to me.

We all love elephants and surely we all wish for a healthy future for them. Let us do all we can to conserve them – that is certainly what I feel about them when I think about African elephants while at home in Scotland. However, if I were to see one ripping up a tree on the edge of my own children's school playground, I might feel slightly differently about their place in our community. I might weigh up the pros and cons of the conservation of elephants in my area against the health and safety of our children. There are no easy answers to this: we certainly need to look after the animals of this Earth and the environments in which they live, but decisions on such matters must be led by local communities rather than the wealthy living far away, whose school playgrounds have never been visited by anything more threatening than a squirrel. We long ago killed all the bears and wolves that roamed the forests that used to surround our villages, before we chopped all those forests down. Hypocrisy and vested interests challenge us as we strive to look after our global abode.

Although questions relating to the environmental crisis are complex, and opinions on solutions varied, it feels as if there is a profound denial in the hearts of many of us in the West. Perhaps that stems from a deep fear that when we fully acknowledge the cause and effect of this crisis we will be led to some very uncomfortable places. Ultimately, we might need to alter our expectations and our sense of entitlement to the type of lifestyles to which we've become accustomed. We might need to confront the idea of fewer overseas holidays and beef burgers; of more cycling to work and locally grown food. We may need to seriously consider giving some things up. Because if our love prompts us to act charitably towards people who are separated from us by vast distances, it will also extend to future generations. If we desire to share the bread that belongs to all through works of charity, we may recognise that that 'all' includes those coming after us. If we want to give away what is not ours to keep, we might realise that unless we can break free from the consumerism to which we seem to be collectively addicted we will be unable to do so; and instead we will become thieves, stealing the future of our children – and our children's children – in order to satisfy our greed. Environmentalism is, first of all, a matter of justice.

The justice and charity that lead us to share with the poor is the same charity that will lead us to make choices that will help alleviate the damage being done to our planet and help heal it. Because both begin and end in the same place. Both will ask us the same questions: How much am I willing to give up for the greater good? Could I choose to live more simply so that others can simply live? These are questions about charity just as much as they are questions about environmentalism. And charity will tell us that we cannot pursue an environmental agenda that would sacrifice the needs of today's poor. We cannot forget about the scandal of today's poverty – any meaningful solutions to this crisis must involve both ecological and social dimensions. Technology and science have a huge part to play but so does the human heart, for it is there that the desire to change must be born.

Questions about how to protect our environment and more justly use the Earth's resources need to be asked at an international level; they should be posed to and by our politicians and they should challenge the leaders of business. But first we need to ask them of ourselves, and make personal choices that will point to the choices we would like those leaders to make. Because, with every type of charity, but perhaps especially this one, we sometimes prefer to talk about it than to actually do it. I for one am guilty. Not all of us are called to become politically active in regard to this, but none of us are exempt from making some choices about our way of life.

Whether we are striving to be kind neighbours or good stewards of creation, little acts of love are the most important acts of all. And these can lead us to a sense that all of our goods – even the property we have a right to – are in fact fundamentally gifts. The belongings restored to their rightful owner at the 'Buy Your Own' stall are no longer only returned property – they are gifts too. Not the same, perhaps, as the gratuitously given bananas and biscuits, but now gifts none the less: something given us freely, something we are stewards of – each one of us – more than we are owners. Things given for the good of all of us, not just a few of us.

But here we move towards things of faith and the question of who might have provided us with all these things, and who might have inscribed these yearnings for justice and truth and charity in our hearts, and I would prefer to leave them for a little while at least.

All of these works – basic charity, human development, justice, care of the environment and political activism – when healthy, will have the same source and goal: a love for the suffering person that desires them to be immediately relieved of their suffering and liberated for ever from anything that prevents their growth, freedom and joy. As individuals we are each called to serve charity in a unique way. Perhaps as we journey on we will at certain times engage in different forms of charity – or works that grow out of her and remain informed by her. As we do, we should respect and cherish all of those other varieties of healthy charity without seeing them as rivals or in opposition to our own particular mission.

But one day we may find ourselves at a different junction, where we can choose to take a road to a place called Ideology, with streets named things like Karl Marx Road, The Free Market and New Liberalism Town. When we are tired of the sight of human suffering, the anguished cries of the hungry, the growing chasm between the rich and poor and the failure of various attempts to address blatant injustice, this destination beckons us in. This is a place that at last offers some solutions; a place where we can rely on our own thinking and work with all our strength to create a new order in the world, where there is no more chronic hunger and no more abject poverty. If we decide to make our home here, putting ourselves entirely at the service of a political idea or some human thinking, we choose at that point to abandon our journey in pursuit of charity. We might still engage in acts of charity, and the ideas which we now devote ourselves to might not be wholly bad, but we have at this point chosen a different way. And some of those ideologies will articulate clearly their condescension towards charity, viewing it as an outdated, antiquated nuisance soon to be got rid of. It's not a part of town I like very much, but settling there for a while doesn't make you a bad person and it isn't a walled city – hopefully you will be free to leave at some point if you ever wish to.

Even a rudimentary knowledge of the gulags, the self-induced famines, the cults of personality and the concentration camps should persuade us against the folly of throwing ourselves totally at the mercy of someone's new, world-changing idea. And surely the most recent global financial meltdown in the first decade of this century, which the economists and politicians were unable to see coming, let alone prevent, should show us once again that the eradication of poverty cannot be left to market forces alone, as illustrated by the growing queues outside soup kitchens in some of the world's richest nations. Market forces might create wealth for some people – even many people – but left to their own devices, they can never possibly bring about the end of hunger and the suffering of the poor. The market needs to be guided by the wisdom of charity and truth just like the rest of us. In the same way, advances in technology and scientific discoveries can play a hugely important part in creating a better future for all – but not on their own. Technology, of itself, does not wish to serve the poorest of the poor or regulate its own use for the good of all people. Scientific knowledge, as we know only too well, can be used to enable better lives, or can just as easily be used to destroy lives. To leave a better human future in the hands of capitalism, science and technology alone would be like removing our children from our family home and entrusting their care to 'experts' – perhaps the finest investment banker, biochemist or software engineer we can find. I have nothing against any of those professions, but being very good at them has no bearing whatsoever on being a good parent. For raising children is first of all a work of love, and to do it well requires a set of moral values and deep commitment to the value of relationship. Those attributes are no more likely to be found in a leading global economist than in the treasurer of our local football club. To disconnect decisions about the fate of humanity from truth and charity, preferring instead to trust the experts in economics, technology and science – or even a self-proclaimed expert in international development – would be a catastrophic mistake, one that could only happen if we ever lost sight of the wonder of the human person and the idea of transcendent truth and became limited to seeing progress only in terms of economy, utility, materialism and technology. If they are the sum of our existence then, yes, let's hand over our entire future to the experts in those things. That would be logical. But if we are more than that, and if there is a truth that exists before us and outside of us, please let's not rush headlong over that cliff.

A troubled government minister of an impoverished African nation once spoke to me about the huge pressure being exerted on him and his government by some in the international community. Representatives of donor governments and international bodies were explicitly telling them that some desperately needed aid agreements under discussion were dependent upon that African government implementing certain policies to which they were fundamentally opposed – policies relating to abortion law and population control (population control being another 'modern wisdom' of the rich, who perhaps prefer the idea of fewer people to less consumerism, and who pedal the dangerous oversimplification that the planet is groaning under the weight of too many people rather the weight of their own shopping baskets). The African politician was someone who had his own strong idea of transcendent truth on such matters – and that truth held much greater sway over him than even the dangling of money that could alleviate the suffering of his own people. I hope those who were exerting that pressure thought they were doing so for the greater good, but even if they were, surely, they should have understood that just because they happened to have more money, it didn't mean they had more truth. Regardless of personal beliefs, to trample on people's ethics and culture in such a way represents the worst type of imperialism imaginable. Matters like these must always be for a sovereign nation to freely decide upon. Those using 'aid' in such a way have long since left behind charity and truth and have chosen instead to try to impose their own ideologies upon vulnerable people. The idea that charity or development is about transforming poor countries into replicas of Western countries is a perverse one: one that fundamentally distorts the essence of charity. It is also a notion that displays a profound lack of respect for all that is good about the people and the cultures of those countries, and one that must be based on a very strange presumption that Western countries have all the answers. Surely even the briefest glance at our daily news bulletins tells us we haven't. To think that the best a society could ever aspire to is a replication of our own represents a remarkable lack of imagination and ambition.

People who hold the strings of enormous purses, experts in technology and leading scientists offer us things that shine ever more brightly – things that can be hard to resist. They can become so dazzling they can blind us, if we are not careful, to the majesty and beauty of the human person.

People of charity cannot choose to ignore the injustices that condemn people to lives of suffering and poverty. Our love will make us want to see the rights of people upheld and their dignity respected. We want to see the walls that entrap them – and the ceilings that prevent their escape – smashed to smithereens. But that does not mean every organisation should engage in every type of good work. We need to discern what is ours to do and what is best left to others.

And this leads us back to the importance of charitable organisations being very clear about their mission and the values that guide it. In the face of all these interconnected needs and our desires to meet them, in different ways, the choices become numerous. If we do not possess a deep, shared understanding of where our mission starts and stops, we will revisit the same debates repeatedly, and our inconsistent decision-making will allow things to drift who knows where. And if we add to that a belief that the *way* we do things is as important as the end results, then more than ever we need to engage in some celestial cartography and start mapping those stars in a way that allows them to guide us.

Each organisation will need to do this work itself and formulate something that can act as a sure guide for its own unique mission. Otherwise it will end up only trying to mimic something that looks older and wiser and more successful – but that path leads only to a painful identity crisis.

The oldest humanitarian organisation – and by some measures the largest – the International Red Cross, long ago mapped its guiding stars and called them its 'Fundamental Principles'. These were proclaimed in 1965, although they had been formulated and written many years previously. The seven Fundamental Principles are:

- Humanity
- Impartiality
- Neutrality
- Independence
- Voluntary Service
- Unity
- Universality

Each of these is clearly defined and together they provide a framework that holds the vast organisation together in an ever-changing world.

Many other organisations that have stood the test of time and continued to flourish through different generations have done something similar. Other well-known organisations seem to have done less well in this task, however, allowing themselves to be changed to reflect the views of their latest leader or a current popular ideology, rather than staying true to the original mission and intention of its founders.

Amnesty International was founded in 1961 to fight for human rights by highlighting the plight of prisoners of conscience and issuing a compelling call to justice and direct action. In 2011, during a radio programme marking Amnesty's fiftieth anniversary, the BBC's Sir John Tusa encapsulated the nature of its work as follows:

An ordinary citizen sits in an ordinary home, writing an extraordinary letter on behalf of somebody they don't know, to a dictator who doesn't care. The letter says: 'We know you have imprisoned X … Be warned. We will go on writing until you have freed them.'

It is a compelling and easily understood mission, admired and supported by millions of people of good will, regardless of their own political persuasion or religious belief. But in the years since Amnesty International has broadened and changed their focus quite dramatically. On their website, a section headed 'Amnesty evolves' states:

> Over the years, human rights have moved from the fringes to centre stage in world affairs. Amnesty has grown from seeking the release of political prisoners to upholding the whole spectrum of human rights. Our work protects and empowers people – from abolishing the death penalty to protecting sexual and reproductive rights, and from combatting discrimination to defending refugees and migrants' rights. We speak out for anyone and everyone whose freedom and dignity are under threat.

This shift has seen the organisation take a position on a whole number of very divisive issues. For example, they played a lead role in campaigning for the legalisation of abortion in Ireland in the lead-up to the 2018 referendum on the matter, including the funding of an TV advert which was described by Tim Stanley in the *Daily Telegraph* as 'blatantly anti Catholic'. Regardless of our personal views on the rights of the unborn child, or on matters of faith, I wonder what Peter Beneson, the Catholic who founded Amnesty International, would feel about its evolution in the years since and whether, with the wisdom of hindsight, he might have chosen to have spent more time 'mapping the stars' in a way that might have helped guard against potential, spectacular mission drift and the alienation of many long-term supporters.

Mary's Meals is very small indeed compared to the Red Cross or Amnesty International, but because we hope this work might continue to grow and flourish long after those of us who founded it, we are doing our best to formulate our equivalent of the Fundamental Principles. Some years ago we wrote our mission, vision and values statement and we continue to work to bring them to life to ensure they never become just clichéd posters in our offices, but remain something alive and at the core of our mission. We want them to be understood, loved and lived in a particular way by our leaders. We say that the way we do things is as important as the end results and we believe that unique way can only be cultivated by taking time to ensure we understand why we approach things in a certain way. So, for example, the most senior staff in the organisation are paid salaries lower than those in equivalent roles in other organisations. This is not because we have failed to 'keep up', but is the result of a policy which derives from our core values, which expect that those privileged enough to be paid for working for Mary's Meals have a vocational attitude, and that high salaries will not become a barrier to them sitting down to break bread with their co-workers in the world's poorest countries, or donors who share with us from their state pensions, or the tens of thousands of volunteers who receive no financial reward for their labour in service of our mission, and that they will be happy to look them in the eye as they do so.

This is a hard one to live out: sometimes fantastic candidates cannot come to work for us because of their financial commitments; sometimes it takes us longer to find the person with the required skills. However, we find that our stubborn adherence to this policy attracts some amazing leaders – people who are choosing to make financial sacrifices to come and work with us because they love our mission so deeply. And they can be the very best of leaders.

The 'Mary's Meals Way' includes some other unusual approaches. While we see the necessity of planning in order to be good stewards, we are reluctant to become driven by numeric targets. We do not want them to become a measure of success or failure, nor do we wish to create another pressure that might erode an approach to fundraising that could be described as 'gentle' and which puts respect for the donor at its heart. And, more fundamentally, we want to retain a recognition that this mission of ours is not entirely within our control; that we are serving something much bigger than us. That is something we can think of in different ways according to our different beliefs – that bigger thing we serve might be the enormous and growing 'movement' of participants in the mission, it might be God Himself, or it might be both. Whether we choose to call it 'divine providence' or the 'wonder of humanity' we can see that things we never could have expected or would have dared to write down in a plan keep surprising us, over and over again, in ways that would make it difficult for any of us to really believe that we are completely in control of things or that we ourselves are the prime movers.

Being a diverse family in matters of faith but united in one simple mission is a very beautiful thing, but it can sometimes throw up challenges around identity, culture and use of language. We are called Mary's Meals for a reason – Mary being the mother of Jesus. The story of our birth is intrinsically linked to a story of faith – Christian faith – and our values are shaped and informed by a Christian spirituality which affirms that charity is love, received and given and that true development requires not only technical progress and relationships of utility, but also love; a love that must be rooted, always, in truth, to avoid the risk of becoming something only sentimental.

At the same time, we have always proclaimed that this mission belongs to people of all faiths and none, and that our help to those in need would always be given freely without ever coercing those who accept it into changing their beliefs or creed, or without them ever being judged in some way.

The only qualification required to join our movement is a desire to see hungry children fed and set free from poverty. While we may not all share the same beliefs, we certainly share a love of the children we serve. And as the Mary's Meals movement grows ever more diverse in terms of creed and race and geography, it becomes ever more beautiful and ever more capable of fulfilling our mission and vision.

There is no inherent contradiction in a mission being a universal one, welcoming and serving all, while also being one that is informed and shaped by a particular faith. And it certainly isn't unusual. Just a cursory glance at any list of the world's largest and most loved charitable organisations reveals how many of them have a similar story. But it can certainly create a tension that needs to be held very carefully. Ensuring that no one is alienated and that all feel equally valued while safeguarding the core identity and ethos of the organisation is not always straightforward – especially at a time when in the

West public expressions of faith are often frowned upon by a society being shaped, at least in part, by an aggressive secularism.

To be true to our mission we might sometimes require a thick skin and a willingness not to 'go with the flow'. When I was a small child, I remember an occasion when, unbeknown to my parents, I crept out of the house with my adventurous elder sister Ruth and her friends and walked quietly to a field where their horses stood. I cannot remember now whether we actually rode the horses in that midnight hour (that, I think, had been Ruth's intention). What I do remember is lying on the bare back of our stumpy little Highland pony and staring at the stars for a long time. My sister and her friends taught me the names of some of the constellations. I was enthralled as I traced the imaginary shapes they drew in the black sky: the Plough, the Seven Sisters, Orion and his belt. Some of their names and the stories attached to them have their origins in pre-history, and yet we learn them again, each new generation.

If we find ourselves entrusted with being stewards and leaders of a charitable mission, let's take some time to learn about the constellations that guide us. Let us delight in those stars and not become beguiled by others that may sometimes gleam brighter, but which cannot become a map for our particular journey. Let's become so familiar with our own constellations that we could ride our horse through the blackest of nights without going astray and find ourselves still galloping on the road of our choosing the next morning, as the first light from the rising sun heralds the gift of a new day.

7

Without Trumpets

You pray for the poor and then you feed them;
that is how prayer works.

POPE FRANCIS

In those days after the earthquake, Father Tom spoke to me
of his experience in the hours immediately after the catastrophe happened. He described the overwhelming terror and
panic that gripped everyone. He had found himself in a crowd
on the street who were looking to him for leadership and, with
his characteristic humility, he told me of his shame at feeling
just as bewildered and traumatised as those around him.
Eventually he did have an idea.

'Let's go and see the Missionaries of Charity,' he suggested,
and they headed off on the short walk to the sisters'
compound through streets full of dead, injured and grief-
stricken people. The Missionaries of Charity (the order of
nuns established by Mother Teresa) were near neighbours
and on most mornings Father Tom visited to say Mass for
them. Among other works for the poor and destitute, they

cared for about fifty abandoned orphan children and babies who lived with them.

Father Tom told me that when they entered the gates from the street into the compound it was like entering another world. Everything was in order. The dead were laid out in one part of their courtyard. In another, the children in their care were sitting or lying in their cots, having been evacuated from a dormitory which was on the brink of collapse. And in another area the injured were being tended to by the sisters, who seemed to be going about their business as if it were just another day. An air of calm pervaded the place, in stark contrast to the anguished chaos outside.

'It was a real lesson to me in just how rooted those sisters are in prayer,' Father Tom reflected. 'Their faith in God is so deep and solid that not even an earthquake could shake it.'

The Mother Teresa sisters have long fascinated me. During my journeys into charity I have encountered them regularly – usually in places so dark that most would not freely choose to visit them, let alone live in them. Sometimes I have bumped into them by chance; at other times I have sought them out, as Father Tom did that day, because in them I see charity practised in the most extraordinary way.

One of those encounters happened on my first visit to Haiti, in a town called Hinche in the Central Plateau. It was the day we served our very first meals in Haiti, and by chance I bumped into a group of them on the street. We got talking and they explained that it was the anniversary of the death of Mother Teresa and invited me back to celebrate with them. The celebration was short – my time with the malnourished babies in their care much longer. Almost before I realised what had happened, they had me helping them feed the stick-thin, impossibly tiny babies, some of whom looked unlikely to survive the day. What struck me then, and has many times since, was the sense of joy and peace in those sisters as they performed the most mundane tasks. I have had the same type of experience with them in places such as Monrovia, the capital of Liberia, in a remote leper colony in South Sudan and in a bustling slum of Lima in Peru. Once I even had the privilege of making a short visit to their Mother House in Kolkata. Invariably I end up holding a sick child, and, after being beguiled by the sisters and those in their care, I am usually asked for some kind of practical help. The Mother Teresa sisters – and nuns in general – have no shame when it comes to begging on behalf of the poor. And they are extremely hard to say no to.

For a period of time I had to visit Haiti quite frequently, normally travelling from Scotland via an airport in Florida. Invariably I found myself collecting a ridiculously large suitcase from the Missionaries of Charity house in Miami in order to deliver it to their fellow sisters working across the Caribbean waters in Port-au-Prince. This contained medicines and all kinds of precious things that I probably didn't have the right paperwork for. As I lugged it off the conveyor belt in Arrivals and nervously eyed the customs officials ahead, I would moan and try to remember when and why I had agreed to do this.

The order of the Missionaries of Charity was founded by Mother Teresa in 1950 in Calcutta (today Kolkata) when, along with a small group of sister nuns, she began providing hands-on care for the most unloved and uncared-for people in society – especially those shunned by others. Today there are over 5,000 Missionaries of Charity; women who have taken vows of chastity, poverty and obedience (in the same way those joining many other Catholic congregations do), and an additional fourth vow: 'to give wholehearted free service to the poorest of the poor'. Those vows are only taken after nine years of study and formation. Present in most of the world's poorest countries, their little communities serve refugees, former prostitutes, the mentally ill, lepers, people with AIDS, the elderly and abandoned and sick and malnourished children, among others.

They are a very large international organisation by most people's standards. But despite their distinctive garb (which is often how I have spotted them amid a teeming crowd) they are, in many ways, much less visible than many much smaller initiatives. That is by choice. They have no website and several times while with them I have heard them explain to visitors and volunteers that they do not want to be photographed when working with the poor. They do not wish to draw attention to themselves and their approach to fundraising is based on a radical reliance on divine providence (and mainly involves the direct asking of people to give them what they need to care for those they are serving). They themselves each own only three saris (one to wear, one to wash, one to mend), two or three cotton habits, a girdle, a pair of sandals, a crucifix and a rosary. They also each have a plate, a set of cutlery, a cloth napkin, a canvas bag and a prayer book. In cold countries, they may own a cardigan and other articles suited to the local climate such as a coat, scarf and closed shoes.

These are low-maintenance, highly trained (how many of us have a nine-year preparation period before we begin our mission?) practitioners of charity. I think of them as being like an elite unit – the Marines or SAS of the charity world perhaps – who can do things the rest of us can only dream of. But that doesn't mean we cannot be inspired by them and learn from them. I might not be able to run vast distances carrying a huge weight of kit and then swim across a lake, but when I look at what those joining the SAS must do, I am both impressed and reminded of the importance of physical fitness – even if that for me means getting back to doing a short daily jog.

The spirituality of Mother Teresa and the life of her sisters has influenced the values and ethos of our own mission and many others. They might be choosing to live an extreme version of charity to which most of us are not called, but in doing so they magnify certain precepts and truths that might help many of us who wish to practise charity better.

First of all, they live very deeply a sense that their work of charity is not about them. When they 'give of themselves' they do not want it announced with a trumpet blast. They hold no desire to be praised or gain status of any sort, as individuals or even as a collective. They want to be little. And they wish all the glory to be given to God.

This can be challenging for those of us taking a different approach to fundraising, which involves us feeling obliged to take every opportunity to raise awareness of the cause and the profile of our mission. I know from personal experience that there is a risk that when we do this, we end up elevating our own status as well that of the organisation we are serving, creating confusion and distraction from the most important things. I have, on occasion, felt keenly the absurdity of being given some personal accolade that would have been much more appropriately shared by every co-worker involved in our work. But then not all of those thousands of people could all at once stand at one podium, grasp the trophy and give a combined acceptance speech. Some things are better done by individuals, as long as they remember they are merely a representative carrying out another act of service. In saying that, the idea of being given a prize for doing something as basic as providing children with a meal continues to feel strange to me. It's not as though every parent or every school dinner lady receives an award for doing the same thing each day.

The glitz and celebrity that can attach itself to aspects of our modern fundraising efforts can become dangerous if we are not very careful. When I began this journey, while driving a noisy, dirty old truck to Bosnia, I did not think it would end up taking me to royal palaces, the Vatican and Hollywood, or that I would meet monarchs, popes and film stars – and there is much of that I have never wished for. In fact, I would have parked the truck and run away if I had suspected that this journey might lead to some of those destinations. But it has happened, and in those places, the truth is I have sometimes made new friends with people who have been able to do wonderful things to help grow our work. And it reassures me to know that even Mother Teresa ended up having to do such things at much more elevated strata of society, and in a much more public way. Becoming a close friend of Princess Diana and being given the Nobel Peace Prize does not seem to have changed in any way the approach of that stubborn, little, sandal-wearing Albanian nun. It seems to me that she tended to have a much greater influence on those she met than they on her. And her acceptance speech for the Nobel Peace Prize demonstrated that universal popularity never became her motivation. Here instead was a sincere expression of her own unchanging beliefs and an example of how deeply rooted she was in who she was – a unique individual clear about her own purpose in life.

'If you are humble nothing will touch you, neither praise nor disgrace, because you know what you are,' she once said, in a statement that gives an insight into how she navigated the minefield of status and human praise, while also shedding light on how her sisters behaved so stoically in the aftermath of the earthquake.

Her sisters also demonstrate the power of simplicity. They live a very simple life indeed. And their mission, too, remains simple – to pray and serve the one in front of them. They decline an engagement with struggles for justice or human development, not because they do not desire those things to happen, but because that is not their calling. They wish to be very good at cleaning the sores of the dying homeless man and at easing his pain. They are not going to launch a campaign to end homelessness, although they will be happy to see others do so. Theirs is an unusual clarity of purpose and simplicity, rooted in a very profound humility: one that lets them see that they are not called to do everything; that they cannot solve all the problems around them; that they are very little and weak in the midst of the sea of suffering they chose to immerse themselves within. But there they can tend to those painful wounds – and for the dying homeless man, who never experienced love like that before, what in all the world could be more important than that?

'Not all of us can do great things. But we can do small things with great love,' Mother Teresa famously remarked. And from the Missionaries of Charity's very deep and particular sense of vocation we can learn other things too. Their founder once joked about this topic, saying, 'I know God won't give me anything I can't handle. I just wish He didn't trust me so much.' On another occasion, when speaking of her motivation, she said something quite revealing about her own natural inclinations and how she overcame them. 'I try to give to the poor people for love what the rich could get for money. No, I wouldn't touch a leper for a thousand pounds; yet I willingly cure him for the love of God.' Maybe we can feel reassured to learn that even a saint like her was not a 'natural' when it came to every aspect of serving, and that the person she became was a product of her choice and discipline rather than her personal likes and dislikes.

And when it comes to trusting in divine providence – an attitude that influences Mary's Meals and many other charities – the Missionaries of Charity have again taken it to an extreme. In fact it has been a source of personal frustration for me at times that they will not accept any support for their mission which requires them to write proposals and reports (making it difficult for an organisation that needs to be accountable to its donors, to make any commitment to fund them). Instead they prefer to rely on the freely given gifts of individuals and it can be seen that this approach is fruitful even if it does test – and then perhaps strengthen – their faith frequently.

It seems to me in my encounters with various scattered outposts of their community that Mother Teresa must have done a great job of 'mapping the stars' during her lifetime. I am sure many entrepreneurs and CEOs of large businesses would love to know how to achieve that clarity of mission, unity of purpose and consistency of culture. They would have been delighted to have created such a powerful brand. (I imagine Mother Teresa never thought about branding but the strikingly simple white sari, bordered by blue stripes, is certainly an evocative and iconic image.)

But if you asked any of Mother Teresa's sisters today how they have managed to become like this, I think it unlikely they would talk about their strategic planning, their research and development or their talent recruitment. They would instead, invariably, point to God and to their daily prayer routine as the source of their strength. And in that they are not alone.

Barcelona, Spring 2018

Marta knows how to prioritise. Our first stop during our hectic four-day schedule in Spain – which she has prepared meticulously – has us driving directly from El Prat airport in Barcelona to visit a group she describes as our most passionate and important supporters in the country. We arrive early and ring the doorbell of a house adjoining a church. A voice welcomes us in and asks us to wait while our hosts finish their lunch. We stand in a bare parlour until, after a few silent minutes, some large shutters open, revealing a wrought-iron grille behind which some smiling faces begin to appear – faces framed by the distinctive white habits of nuns. A dozen of them live here, belonging to the centuries-old Carmelite order and choosing to live a life dedicated to prayer and contemplation enclosed behind the grilles and doors of their convent.

They thank us profusely for coming to visit and tell us of their love for Mary's Meals. They explain that their daily routine involves one of them reading a book to the others while they eat their lunch, and that recently they read my book about Mary's Meals in that manner. And they explain that they pray for us every day. Deeply moved, I thank them, telling them that they are a much-valued and beautiful part of our mission. One of them, with a young beaming face, steps forward from the shadows and shyly tells us that she had first learnt of Mary's Meals a few years previously when, prior to being an enclosed nun, she had attended the huge annual youth festival in Medjugorje where she had heard us speak about our work from the stage. We chat for a few more minutes, our conversation punctuated by lots of laughter, and then they ask me a favour. To the side of the grille a little turntable creaks and begins to revolve (their method of passing items in and out of their enclosed convent) and a slightly worn copy of my book appears with a request for me to write a note on it for them. I do so and send it back the way it came. Another creak, and an envelope appears in front of me which I discover later contains an incredibly generous donation.

I leave feeling very blessed by the visitation, which evoked memories of some Carmelite nuns I knew growing up. They were dear friends of my grandmother and sometimes we used to visit them. Later, when we first began to drive aid to Bosnia, they prayed and prayed for us. We depended on them a lot. When that particular convent finally closed down they donated to us everything in it, and we loaded much of what they gave us into our truck and drove to Bosnia.

These Spanish Carmelites felt like a key part of our new presence in Spain and the whirlwind tour of the country that followed – giving talks to full churches in Barcelona, Madrid, Seville and Valencia – felt deeply blessed. Many new people volunteered to help us and a vibrant new group began forming in each city.

Prayer has so often come first in the story of Mary's Meals. In our mission statement we describe prayer as one of the gifts people can offer Mary's Meals and often when I am speaking about our work, I describe it as 'a fruit of prayer'. That remains my personal conviction.

I have encountered a startling variety of people praying for our work over the years. Just a couple of weeks before my visit to those nuns in Barcelona I had been invited to speak to a youth prayer group in Paris. A group of sixty or seventy gathered in a crypt below their parish church, as they did every week, to praise God. For two hours they sang praise songs and danced for joy – trendy teenagers, dancing without inhibition and not a drop of alcohol to be seen, just a faith that seemed to fill them with immense joy. The same thing, but on a vast scale, occurs each year at the youth festival in Medjugorje, when tens of thousands of youngsters gather from over 100 countries to pray and celebrate their joyful faith. This probably also represents the biggest gathering of Mary's Meals supporters each year – as can be seen in the smattering of bright blue Mary's Meals T-shirts everywhere in the enormous crowd. These days act as a reminder to us – if any were needed – that many involve themselves in our mission as an expression of their faith. Back in our Glasgow office – a place of fast-paced work where the pressure of supporting this ever-growing global movement can sometimes weigh heavy – some staff gather each morning at 9 am to pray together. And just across the road from my office in the 'shed', the little faith community at Craig Lodge Family House of Prayer make the 'Mary's Meals Prayer' part of their daily devotions.

The place of prayer can also be central to the relationship between Mary's Meals and the impoverished communities we serve. Once I visited a mountaintop school in Haiti, far from any road, where Mary's Meals had just begun. I was there with the Hollywood film star Gerard Butler, who had come to make a new film about our work and thus help us raise awareness. We had climbed with the community – and their donkeys laden with our food – up the steep path to their village. We spent some time chatting to the volunteers as they stirred the beans and rice, asking them about their lives and their motivation to give up their time for this work. At one point, Gerard asked them about how they perceived Mary's Meals and those people in faraway places who were helping provide the food they were cooking. After a little silence an older lady responded.

'Mary's Meals for us is an answer to prayer. We have been praying and praying that God would help us in this situation with our children and then suddenly, boom! – Mary's Meals arrives.'

I have often heard Mary's Meals described as an answer to prayer. And often prayer is the most precious thing those communities can offer us – their co-workers in faraway lands.

In South Sudan, we are welcomed in schools with wonderful songs and dances – and prayer too. On one occasion I arrived there with my co-worker Alex. We were both feeling quite unwell, having picked up some kind of illness in Madagascar a couple of days earlier. We were struggling a little to stand in the baking heat of the playground as each class trooped out to encircle us with their vigorous welcome. After a short speech, two pupils emerged from their ranks; one stood in front of each of us and placed their hands gently on our foreheads (which they could only just reach when we bowed a little). For some time they prayed for us in silence. It was a beautiful, unexpected thing to arrive in that place of war and endemic violence and be ministered to in that way by children: yet again, as we went about our work of giving, we ended up receiving too.

And my experience of prayer in this work doesn't confine itself to the Christian variety. I treasure the precious time spent in prayer with those of other faith traditions. Mary's Meals has been welcomed into the heart of many Muslim communities – for example in the remote villages of Cape Mount, Liberia. While setting up new projects there we would often work with the local Imam and each community meeting would start with heartfelt prayer together. There was no awkwardness in these villages at the idea of Christians and Muslims praying together – it was just the most natural way for them to begin any such gathering.

And it is not only in the places where we serve meals that Mary's Meals draws those from different faiths together. I have seen various ecumenical and interfaith initiatives find their common ground in the service of this mission. In

Dundee, Scotland, a group of women, saddened by difficult relationships between the various faith communities in their city, decided to stage a Mary's Meals event aimed at raising some funds for us – but also with the purpose of bringing these groups together. The exuberant email rushed out to us straight after the event by Claire, one of the organisers, painted a wonderful picture:

> We had some additional surprises like a piper who turned up to play and the Sisters of Immaculate Mary who took to the stage and praised the Lord Nigerian style – who needs Whoopi Goldberg – they brought the house down! The Hindu community brought classical Indian dance, with a lovely lady who told the story of the dance and some Bollywood dancers!! In between was Mr Gopal – a lovely chap from the Hindu community – who blessed us with his view of karma and the fact that we all answer to our God in the end. No one could argue with that! We had a fantastic Christian message from Rev Robert, a fabulous local young jazz band and the University of Dundee Traditional Trio to finish.
>
> The buffet was 100% donation and what a feast – the food left over was donated to Jericho House. We have raised over £700 already, which is amazing as I gave so much away. I know some of your donators make more, but what has happened here has been God changing. I can't begin to tell you the ingrained differences your lovely charity has turned on its head. So many young people were there on Sat eve and want more. Hallelujah and praise our Lord Jesus for that.

PS I didn't say but 2 Muslim men turned up – just for 10 mins because it's Ramadan – but they came!!

Lots of wonderful humanitarians, including many of my own co-workers and close friends, are not people of faith – and some of them are among those I have learnt most from in this journey. To foster the place of faith and prayer within a mission consisting of people of all sorts of backgrounds and faiths requires much sensitivity and thoughtfulness by all concerned. There are various risks attached: one is that some wear their faith on their sleeves in a way that alienates or discourages those who do not share their beliefs. Another danger – which can result from well-meaning attempts to mitigate the first risk – is the prohibition of expressions of faith within the mission. It is worth huge effort, much dialogue and the taking of some risks to avoid either of these grave mistakes.

Our respect for each other's different beliefs should not need to result in a form of charity that eliminates the place of faith when it is so central for so many people and their communities. Authentic charity acknowledges and respects the whole person and is aware of the various needs a person has – not only the material and physical ones. That does not mean we all need to become priests or psychologists, but because charity seeks the very best for the person it serves it will want to understand the things most important in that person's life.

Towards the end of the wars in the former Yugoslavia I was struck by a thank-you letter we received from our longstanding Croatian partner organisation there, The Family Centre

(SIR stands for Scottish International Relief, the first organisation we founded).

28 February 2000

Dear Friends in Scotland

We from Croatia wish to express our deep gratitude for your part in so important and helpful work of SIR in Croatia, Bosnia, Kosovo and Albania.

Your work, and work of people similar to you, is why life is still beautiful on this earth. Your love and care make difference in lives of many people. Many people in their sufferings experience through your work that there are people who care enough to do something for them. Your help is not only material but also psychological. People are encouraged, hope is renewed and they because of your kindness are kind to other people.

For those with the gift of Faith your efforts and love is one more sign of God's presence in people and in the world.

Thank you
Marijo Zivkovic, Director

Not long before receiving that letter I had visited a little village in Croatia called Crno, which, like many others, had been destroyed during the war and its people forced to flee. It was the week before Easter and my visit took place because the war was coming to an end and the original inhabitants were now beginning to return in order to try to rebuild their shattered lives. Every home was a roofless, charred mess. As we drove into the pitiful little hamlet, I wondered how the returning inhabitants would find the strength to begin again, and where they would start this daunting task. But it turned out they had a very clear idea about that. In the centre of the village was their little stone church. It was roofless, like every other building. But inside was a hive of activity. The people were clearing the debris of the collapsed roof from the church. This is where they chose to begin, before even touching their own ruined homes. When they celebrated the Resurrection a week later on Easter Sunday, the little congregation still had the sky as their ceiling, but the floor was swept clean and vases of bright flowers adorned the little altar.

In the weeks after, as we accompanied them by sending truck-loads of aid from Scotland, in addition to their requests for practical things – food, tools and cutlery – they asked us for items to refurbish their beloved little church. At the same time, back in Scotland, churches and convents were closing for other reasons and sometimes offering us their most precious contents. And so in the back of our trucks as they rumbled across Europe, amid the hammers, saws and kitchen knives could sometimes be found candlesticks and crucifixes (there was even an organ from our friends the Carmelite nuns in Oban).

The sending of such goods prompted some debate in our organisation. Were we diluting our non-denominational approach? Could we be accused of proselytising? After all, we had been clear from the outset that we were a universal mission, welcoming and serving all regardless of their creed.

We were adamant that our help would always be freely given and never used to coerce people in matters of faith or any other matter related to personal belief – and that remains a cornerstone of our approach to this day. It is one of the 'guiding stars' we navigate by and is clearly articulated in our statement of values.

But we kept sending those religious items when asked and when they happened to be donated to us, because we saw they were very precious indeed for those traumatised people – a huge aid to them on their road to rehabilitation and peace. They were not being used by people to evangelise, but to live out their centuries-old faith in the way they had always done before being 'ethnically cleansed'.

Charity is interested in the whole person, not just a part of them. While we cannot be experts in every aspect of humanity, and while we should not lose sight of the importance of humility when discerning what we can and cannot do, a recognition that human needs are not only confined to material things is important. And those needs are present in the humans who support charity as well those who receive it. So often giving is an expression of faith. Even an organisation that is not attached to a particular creed, or belonging to a particular church, can recognise and respect (and even celebrate) that in the people they serve.

That 'holistic' approach can be a challenging one. It can lead us to ask questions of ourselves about the way in which we give. When Mother Teresa said: 'There is more hunger for love and appreciation in this world than for bread,' she was echoing the famous words of Jesus when He asserted that 'man shall not live by bread alone.' (Matthew 4:4, ESV) She was reminding us that the person in front of us is not only one with a stomach, but one with a mind, heart and soul too. Sometimes it is not enough to meet the material needs – to throw the food off the back of the truck and leave. There are much deeper human wants that can only be met by the giving of time – by listening and sometimes speaking, by expressing empathy and demonstrating solidarity. For some of us this is a much harder kind of charity than the fast-paced, problem-solving type. Not all of us, obviously, are called to become nuns or people involved in hands-on care, spending hours each day spoon-feeding a malnourished child, or speaking words of love to the lonely person suffering from AIDS who has already lost all her children to the same disease. But we can all make time each day for those around us – our co-workers, our supporters, the people we are serving. We can take opportunities, even if they are limited, to speak with them and get to know them – to make friends with them even. When we fail to do that our efforts can no longer be called a work of love, because we are no longer giving of ourselves. Giving gifts, yes, but our very selves, no.

If we desire that – to give not just a material gift but to give of ourselves – we can find ways to do so even when our charitable effort is simply making a donation. There are ways to make it personal if we wish it to be.

Even the simple question of 'how much' can enable us to do that. C. S. Lewis, in his book *Mere Christianity*, wrote:

I do not believe one can settle how much we ought to give. I am afraid the only safe rule is to give more than we can spare. In other words, if our expenditure on comforts, luxuries, amusements, etc, is up to the standard common among those with the same income as our own, we are probably giving away too little. If our charities do not at all pinch or hamper us, I should say they are too small. There ought to be things we should like to do and cannot do because our charitable expenditure excludes them.

Mother Teresa said it another way: 'Give, but give until it hurts.'

There are other ways too, for us be creative about 'giving of ourselves' when those we are helping are too distant for us to speak with or hug.

One morning in the spring of 2018 our postman delivered to us a thick and heavy A4-sized envelope. I could see from the stamp that it was from Innsbruck and felt intrigued. I had only been to that city once before and could not immediately think of anyone I knew there. Inside was a letter from a Mrs Marihart explaining that she had attended an event the previous year in a book shop in Innsbruck, where I had given a presentation about Mary's Meals. She explained that a couple of days later, while she was digging her garden and thinking about how she could help us feed more children, her spade hit something hard. She unearthed a small cross and, although describing herself as 'not very religious', felt this somehow to be significant.

She was a teacher and immediately she began fundraising in her school community for one child to be fed for a year. And then another – and another. Every time someone donated the cost of feeding another child, she wrote the story of that donation beneath a stencil drawing of a child, with a name she had given it (often linked to the story). The envelope was a heavy one because her letter contained the news that she had just collected enough donations to feed 500 children, and inside were pages filled with stories and colourful pictures of children; tales of friends sewing quilts, teachers baking, children making toy elephants and some funny stories too, such as one in which she described being pulled over by a policeman for speeding and eventually persuading him to make a donation to feed another child!

A couple of months later I was giving a little talk at our 'leadership academy' (when each year another cohort of our senior staff leaders gather from different parts of the world for a training course aimed at helping them become better leaders in general, and better 'Mary's Meals leaders' in particular). That theme was stewardship and I chose to devote my entire twenty-minute slot to reading out Mrs Marihart's letter and the story of each donation. It felt like there could be no better way to be reminded of the preciousness of each child – and the preciousness of each gift.

She had written:

Every little scene I told you about Mary's Meals makes me feel happy. These are tiny scenes but really heartlifting scenes. It is not the real 'big money' that a very rich person would be able to give you. But I think every Euro counts, and every girl or boy that is not hungry any more and can go to school counts. In my mind I see 500 kids looking into a better future.

And then in December another similar-looking parcel was
delivered to our door. This time it contained the news that she
had collected enough donations to feed 1,000 children, and
again was filled with stencil drawings of the additional 500
children and the story of each donation that had made it
possible. These anecdotes were sometimes mundane, but in
their telling there were glimpses of the length Mrs Marihart
was going to in order to reach the next child and how she was
managing to involve ever-increasing numbers of people in her
mission.

Sultan, my Turkish girlfriend, works in a senior citizens'
home. She does not have really much money, but when
she saw my shell-pillows that I wanted to sell for Mary's
Meals she said 'Please sell them to me so I have a nice
birthday present from my sister and her friend – 4 kids.'
   My pupils from class 2 wanted to do a next special
event for Mary's Meals. So I sew morsbags and lanyards
to sell them in front of the local supermarket. It was a
real pleasure to watch them talking about Mary's Meals
… asking for a donation or just selling morsbags and
lanyards. I was astonished at how polite and friendly they
were. I was smiling all over my face! How for example
Lena – at first shy and not speaking, grew and found
more confidence to speak to persons she did not know
before. Standing for the project Mary's Meals makes her
standing a little but stronger in her life – 9 kids.

And then there was another story involving her car. This time it had been vandalised along with ten other cars overnight. She reported it and some days later the police contacted her to say that a 'young contrite man, who has been really drunk this evening' and couldn't even remember that he had caused the damage until his friends told him, had confessed his crime and offered the money required to do the repairs. Mrs Marihart wrote him a letter via the police, congratulating him on his honesty, explaining that her insurance would cover her costs, telling him about Mary's Meals and suggesting that if he wished he could make a donation. And that's what he did, transferring it to her bank account along with his full name – '7 kids.'

> So, dear Mr Magnus, I hope you enjoyed the new stories,
> I will continue to help you feed the boys and girls
> somewhere in the world. And I will continue to tell your
> story. Thank you so much that I am able to be a member
> of the Mary's Meals Family.

Another way to give of ourselves, and to place ourselves in solidarity with the poor and hungry is through fasting. This ancient practice is to be found in every world religion – usually as a way to learn bodily discipline and to grow closer to God. At least in the West, this practice, once so prevalent in the Church, has largely been lost. But the idea of fasting as an act of solidarity and sharing is one that is attracting some in the modern world – the religious and the non-religious too. I have seen individuals and groups choose to fast in various ways for Mary's Meals. Sometimes this can involve sharing the money saved by spending less on food so that those suffering chronic hunger might eat. Some undertake total fasts for twenty-four hours. Others skip a meal each day for a period of time. A group of Scottish university students ate nothing but beans for a week. A co-worker of mine, when she began working for Mary's Meals, learnt that many of the children we serve do not eat anything in the morning before walking (often long distances) to school. So she decided to fast for sixteen hours (from the evening before and then skipping breakfast the following morning). She set out to do it for a few days in order to understand better the experience of those children, and to be in solidarity with them. But those few days became a few weeks, and then a few months – and, eventually, a way of life. She continues to make it her daily practice. Her courageous choice means that this work – even amid the daily stresses of life in our office – remains for her a profound work of love.

Some of us, whether we fast or not, find our strength in prayer. When our hearts seem too small and we are ashamed at our lack of love, we can in this way ask for 'new hearts' of flesh to replace our stony ones. Weariness can be overcome – or at least endured – and new vigour found. When we are tempted to give up on something, or when we feel we have nothing left to give, prayer might remind us that things don't depend on us entirely. Our load may start to feel a little lighter.

The morning after Father Tom had told me about his encounter with the sisters in the aftermath of the earthquake, I spent some time with them myself. We chatted briefly in their courtyard (I may have had another large suitcase to deliver to them) after an early morning Mass, while around us

Port-au-Prince was coming to life as survivors were waking up and trying to comprehend that the earthquake and its aftermath hadn't just been a very horrible dream. I mentioned to them Father Tom's recounting of the hours after the earthquake and we began to talk about their experience.

'But were you not scared at all?' I found myself asking them.

'Oh yes, at one point we really were,' one of them said with a smile.

'A little while after the main earthquake had finished there were some terrible aftershocks. Our children at that point were all still inside their house in their cots and a huge crack appeared in the wall. It looked like it was just about to collapse on them. We ran into our little chapel here and fell on our knees. We began begging Jesus to save the children, but the ground kept shaking …' and as she spoke, she surprised me by beginning to cry.

'Then as we prayed our statue of Our Lady in the corner began turning as the ground shook until she was facing Jesus in the tabernacle too. At that very moment the earth stopped shaking.'

By now a few of the sisters were sobbing.

'It was like Mother Mary wanted us to know she was praying with us. Not one of our children were harmed,' they smiled through their tears and headed off to their morning chores and the tending of those children.

Not even the best, most noble doer of charity is without fear, has no problems to overcome, never makes a mistake and has no need of consolation and support. None of us can do this on our own. If we want to make charity a way of life, we need to find a way to receive as well as give. This becomes even more crucial if we want to give of ourselves. The warning light for our fuel tank will start blinking pretty soon if we don't. And if you are a clapped-out old banger like me, you will need not just fuel, but regular maintenance and repair too.

It could be said that charity consists of broken people helping broken people, each becoming a little less broken as they do so. The evening of that same long day in Port-au-Prince, under a tree in Father Tom's courtyard I had opportunity to contemplate that in a new way.

8

Blessed and Broken

Most of us pass our lives away eating the husks of life.
Within them, beneath the rind, is a sweeter fruit than
ever we have tasted. How shall we find it unless the rind
is peeled away by Wisdom greater than our own, by a
Love whose ways are strange and bewildering to us?

SAINT THÉRÈSE OF LISIEUX

In the days after the earthquake, Father Tom's co-workers had
been painstakingly searching the rubble of his collapsed home,
salvaging whatever pitiful belongings they could. When we
returned each evening from the agonised chaotic city to our
makeshift home in the courtyard, the men would show Father
Tom their new haul of recovered objects. One evening they
presented a smashed crucifix. The mangled figure of Christ
was missing parts of its plaster limbs and twisted bits of wire
protruded from the snapped arms and legs. They hung it from
a nail on the tree that had become our makeshift chapel. One
evening, after we had prayed there, Father Tom explained to
me that this crucifix had been a fixture in his family home in

Philadelphia as he grew up. He had been praying in its presence for many years. Recognising its significance to him, I asked him if he might try to have it repaired.

'You know, I actually like it just the way it is,' he replied. 'It reminds me that Jesus is broken too – with us.'

Sooner or later, if we continue to choose certain paths on our journey into charity, we will probably be led to the cross. Not just to those metaphorical crosses relating to our own experiences of suffering, or to symbolic ones like that wrecked one hanging from a tree in Haiti, but – if we are willing to go there – to the foot of the cross on Calvary, confronting us with a tortured, broken Jesus, crying out in anguish as He dies a hideous, humiliating death. If we believe that the smashed-up man hanging from that cross is God, then we are encountering the ultimate and perfect act of charity. Here we might find the answer to our questions. And here we might find our strength, especially when we are most weak – especially when we feel broken. And if even we do not hold a belief in the divinity of Jesus, we still encounter here one whose teachings have informed and inspired charity more than any other.

As we continue our journey from here – and from the empty tomb two days later – we may continue happily to walk the same paths and enjoy each other's company, those of us who believe in this Jesus as God and those of us who do not. And the good works of the believer do not at this point become somehow more valuable than those of the unbeliever. Each continues to hold the same weight regardless of our belief. We may think the dead, tortured young person suspended in front of us was a madman or a liar, and that this whole disturbing scene of brutal execution, cheered on by a blood-crazed mob, was best forgotten long ago along with all the thousands of other crucifixions carried out by the Romans. Or we may gaze on the broken one as our Saviour, and see the blood and water which bursts from the hole punctured by a lance between His ribs as the source of charity, the place from which love flows, never-ending, like a mighty river. Regardless of our differing beliefs, the value of our charity will continue to be dependent only on the amount of love we put into it. However, our understanding of what charity is in essence – the origins of that love and its implications for us as human beings – may diverge at this point, according to our stance on the dead person now being taken down from the cross and laid in His mother's arms. Because if we believe that the tomb in which He was laid was found empty at dawn, two days later, because this Jesus was in fact God – just as He had claimed – then everything changes. Our journey from that point will be forever different because we will be forever different. The ramifications of charity for the believer are now transformed. And because I am one of those believers, this next part of the journey I can only describe through my own paradigm of faith. But I embark on it hoping respectfully that you, my friends with different beliefs, might keep me company as you have done thus far, and that before long we will see our ways continue to converge, in all those acts of love we hold in common, and will continue to complete together.

But, meanwhile, standing with Mary at the foot of that cross on Calvary, we encounter an act of love so outrageous that we could spend a whole lifetime contemplating what occurred on it and still never understand fully or accept it completely, our hearts not being big enough. Here, the believer encounters God giving us His only Son – His beloved Son, so that we might live – the greatest gift that was ever given.

With that final breath breathed in the darkness (although it was the middle of the day it became dark for three hours), Jesus completed the most beautiful and profound act of charity ever made. But even if we believe it – that Jesus died for us personally, offering us a gift so great and so underserved – it can still be a very hard thing to accept it. To accept even a small gift is an uncomfortable experience for many of us. To receive charity is very hard; often much more difficult than providing it for others. Even the thought of asking for help – or even admitting to ourselves we need it – can be too much. How many people have died in despair because they could not say, 'please help me'? Our egos seem to crave self-sufficiency, or at least the appearance of it, sometimes at all costs. But if we do not know how to receive, we do not know how to practise charity.

This in part was one of the lessons Jesus taught His disciples the evening before the horror unfolded on Calvary. During the meal that they were sharing to celebrate the Passover, He scandalised them when he removed His outer garments, wrapped a towel around His waist and prepared to wash their feet. At first a horrified Peter tried to protest: 'Never! You shall never wash my feet.'

But Jesus didn't give way.

'If I do not wash your feet you can have no share with me,' He said.

Peter, being Peter, not only relented – he became passionate in his acceptance.

'Well then, Lord, not only my feet, but my hands and head as well!'

Jesus then duly washed their feet – including those belonging to Judas, the man He knew was about to betray Him to death – and sat back down at the table.

'Do you understand', He said, 'what I have done to you? You call me Master and Lord and rightly; so I am. If I then, the Lord and Master, have washed your feet, you must wash each other's feet. I have given you an example so that you may copy what I have done to you.' (John 13:6–15, NJB)

Thus, Jesus explained what Christians look like; lowly servants carrying out acts of kindness that others disdain. When we complain about our empty churches, the turning away of our young people or the lack of respect shown to our religion we might think about this – about how we as individuals and as a community are acting this out. We might hear in those words of Jesus a call back to the heart of charity – and to the heart of our Christian life.

Even as Jesus continued to speak words of farewell to His confused and frightened friends, He returned once more to this requirement for His followers to imitate Him, going as far as to call it a 'new commandment': 'I give you a new commandment: love one another; you must love one another just as I have loved you.' (John 13:34, NJB)

Of course, we now know what the disciples didn't know that night – that the very next day Jesus was to be crucified out of love for them, and out of love for you and me. It had been horrifying enough to learn that following Him meant washing people's feet and – even worse – allowing them to wash ours. But now we discover a whole new, terrible kind of love to be imitated: the sort that gives up its life for its friends – the sort that even gives up its life for its enemies.

To call oneself a Christian is a brave thing to do. And it is also a very stupid thing to do if we think, that with our own strength, we can honour that commandment of Jesus. That ways leads us, without exception, to abject failure and humiliation – and any sincere Christian journey can only continue in the painfully repeated, ever-growing realisation that we are utterly reliant on God's grace and mercy. And there is a happy paradox: each failure when trying to be a good Christian – each failure when trying to practise charity – is an opportunity for growth, a chance to make progress and a new insight into who we are and who God is. Each time that He picks us up and hugs us, we will know even better how much our Father loves us. Our brokenness is a blessing.

That is why we are at such great risk when our identity becomes all about being the giver; the fixer of other people's problems, the person with all the answers, the indestructible, self-sufficient one. This risk is especially great in the West, where it is written deep into us that we are potential bestowers of gifts. We look at the poor of the world and their need is glaringly obvious. But it can take some digging to recognise that we too have deep needs. Most of our basic needs might be met ... but we certainly *need* them to be met!

A good friend of mine, Maria, spent a number of years with the Franciscan Sisters of the Renewal (CFRs) in New York and Ireland. During 2016, which had been proclaimed as a Year of Mercy by Pope Francis, Maria's community were invited by their spiritual director to reflect on the Works of Mercy and how they could put them into practice more. (The

Works of Mercy are fourteen defined types of charity that Christians are encouraged to practise. The Catholic Church divides them into seven Corporal Works, including feeding the hungry and visiting the sick and seven Spiritual Works, including counselling doubters and comforting the afflicted. The Methodist Church teaches that the works of mercy arc a means of grace which lead to holiness and aid sanctification.) Maria told me she initially found this reflection surprisingly difficult:

> The life of a CFR sister is basically a constant stream of doing works of mercy, yet I had never really reflected on them as 'works of mercy', I just thought of 'serving the poor'. I began trying to be more deliberate in them, but found it wasn't making any differencc to me – it was so much part of my daily life anyway. Something in my heart was saying: I do this stuff all the time (feeding the poor, clothing the homeless, counselling the doubtful, etc); there's nothing more I can add to it. So, I prayed about how I could try to put my heart into it more. I received an answer which deeply changed it for me. I felt drawn to go through the works of mercy and not think about who I was serving, but how I was served in the past, and to think of at least one instance for each work of mercy where I deeply felt my own neediness (for food, shelter, clothing), and to try to recall what it felt like to have deep gratitude welling up because that need was met. I decided the act wouldn't 'count' unless it was an instance of deeply heartfelt gratitude that I experienced.

I can tell you one surprising incident that came back to me: I remembered when my friends got me a T-shirt as a birthday present when I was 15. It was the only trendy thing I owned at the time. It meant so much to me, as shallow as that might sound, but that is the way things work for a teenager! In a sense, they were giving me a share of their own glory, even when I had no means to return it. I knew that they were proud of me and wanted to show it in a gesture of love. If they had tried to get to the roots – interfere with why I wasn't able to afford my own things, I would have felt judged, because those things are complex and not always what they seem. There can be tremendous dignity in the reasons why some people have less – because a family has made costly choices to be generous, because of misunderstandings not easily fixed, sufferings not supported, because ill fortune came along. Sometimes we just need a gift of goodness and kindness that is light-hearted and carries the promise that our desires are heard somewhere in someone's heart, and that they don't presume to judge the intricate and often beautiful strands that cause our own areas of poverty, strands that shouldn't be burst asunder. To know that you are loved and treasured amid the difficulties that you take up as your own responsibility can be a galvanising force.

I was amazed to realise the warmth and light that this continuing spark of gladness about that one little act of love was able to generate! From that point, it was my heartfelt gratitude for this act of love that encouraged me every day that I worked in the clothing pantry to give always the nicest thing I could find to the man or woman who came looking for something. Whether they could sense it or not, I wanted them to be clothed with love and glory like I had once experienced: not so much bodily, but deep in the heart. It was one small act of love from my friends that they probably do not remember ... but it was a little spark capable of sustaining a fire.

Looking at things in this way awoke a new place in my heart to give and act from ... genuine gratitude. It gave me a connection of deep joy that I hadn't experienced before, because suddenly I was doing something as a happy receiver of a gift, not primarily as a principled giver of a gift. It awoke the joy of the conviction: 'this is worthwhile, I remember what a difference it made to me'.

Jesus is the only person who could have been without the needs that Maria speaks of. Before His hands were nailed to the cross they 'moulded our earth', 'threw stars into space' and 'knitted us in our mothers' wombs'. He didn't need anyone's help, yet He chose to put Himself in a situation that allowed people to do whatever they wanted with Him. And when they did, and His awful suffering began, He allowed others to help – Simon Cyrene shouldering His cross, Veronica wiping His bloody face, His mother being there, in His sight as He looked down during three hours of agony.

The only one who isn't dependent shows us that we are. All of us are dependent on each other. All of us are dependent on God, even for our very lives. Each of us is unable to get out of our beds in the morning, never mind carry out an act of charity, by ourselves. Each of us has nothing of our own to give. Jesus' death and resurrection, and a belief in a loving God who created the world, drastically alter our understanding of, and approach to, charity. This doesn't contradict or make worthless the charity of others who do not believe, but it is different nonetheless.

We will know that we are not saviours, for the only Saviour is the one hanging on the cross.

We will know that before we can give, we must receive.

We will know that we are not the prime movers in charity; rather, we are people honoured to work in its service.

We will know that we do not have all the answers, and that the answer to everything is nailed to the tree.

We will know that anything we can give was never ours to keep.

And we will truly know that someone's need never makes them inferior to us, and that our need never makes us inferior to someone else.

We will hear certain questions about sustainability and dependency cultures, and we will laugh at ourselves.

And we will know, too, that even today, when we help someone in need, we help Jesus, just as Simon of Cyrene and Veronica did two thousand years ago. Not long before He was stripped and tortured to death, when talking about how we can gain eternal life, Jesus said:

For I was hungry and you gave me food, I was thirsty and you gave me drink, I was a stranger and you made me welcome, lacking clothes and you clothed me, sick and you visited me, in prison and you came to see me …

In so far as you did this to one of the least of these
brothers of mine, you did it to me. (Matthew 25:34–36,
NJB)

So when we provide a meal for a hungry child, we are feeding a hungry Jesus. When we serve a cup of tea to a homeless
person, we are quenching the thirst of Jesus. When Father
Tom provides school uniforms for the naked street children
of Cité Soleil, he clothes a naked Jesus. When my friend
Graeme volunteers to deliver newspapers to patients in our
local hospital, making time to chat to each, I think he is
visiting Jesus – even if he might not see it that way himself.
Surely those working to welcome newly arrived people from
faraway lands into our country are welcoming Jesus (once a
refugee child Himself), and when I watch some young
French people visiting the children who are suffering without trial inside a prison in Madagascar, I watch people going
to visit Jesus.

What kind of mystery is this, that the only one who doesn't
need our help invites us to help Him? Less of a mystery to the
Christian is what we need to do if we want to gain eternal life.
We have clear instructions on that. God made man, dies for
us and opens the gates, while telling us unequivocally that
entry to heaven is dependent on our practice of charity. Of
course, even then, regardless of what we do, we are completely
reliant on His grace for that too – we cannot save ourselves.
Only God will be our judge, and we can presume He will be
a judge unlike any other we might have encountered.

For in the death of Jesus we see something very strange
happen. Justice is almost turned on its head by God's enor-

mous love for us. Jesus was sacrificed in our place. He died for our sins, not His own. This isn't justice as we know it. Justice should have seen us punished for turning away from God. The way to eternal life should have remained for ever shut to us. Justice should have seen us being handed down a terrible sentence. But the enormity of God's love usurped justice – or at least it found a new way of fulfilling it. Here a new word enters in: mercy. God in His mercy chose to become like a customer at one of those 'Buy your Own' markets in Liberia, paying a high price for things that others had taken from Him rather than pursuing a more obvious justice easily within His power, and then offering them back to the thieves with additional treasure among them. But even that is a pitiful, inadequate analogy. Because what a price He paid!

Even if we can start to accept the concept of what God did, it can be almost too hard to contemplate the way He realised it. To offer to die yourself in place of someone else would be hard enough – but to instead ask your own son to die is something so abhorrent we would rather not contemplate it. And even if we could get to that point, to ask Him to die would be one thing, but to ask Him to be crucified quite another. It is hard to imagine there could be a more horrible way to die. What could be more painful and more humiliating than that? Even 2,000 years later we have not found a stronger word to describe the most extreme kind of pain or torment than 'excruciating', from the Latin *excruciare*.

I am not so foolish as to attempt to explain God's choices when it comes to our salvation. For the purpose of this pursuit of charity I am only attempting to present the enormity of God's love for us and the gift we have first been given – and even that feels well beyond my grasp. But we can see that we have encountered here a perfect love to try to imitate.

'Love one another. As I have loved you, so you must love one another. By this everyone will know that you are my disciples,' said the One whose love for us has Him hanging, broken, from a cross.

This gift of the cross – if we accept that we have been given it – creates a new starting point for our charity. If we recognise that in order to give we must receive, we can see here that we have been given something beyond measure. If we believe and accept the gift – and accept too that everything we will ever have, or be, is a gift – we will have received something that can fuel our giving for a lifetime and more. The more we develop a disposition that treats everything as a gift, the more instinctive and innate our charity becomes. We will feel compelled to share things that were never ours to keep.

On one occasion during the war in the former Yugoslavia we were delivering truck-loads of donated aid to refugees in Zagreb who had just fled from Northern Bosnia. They were in desperate need of even the most basic things. We noticed that as we unloaded the tinned and dried food, they were putting one quarter of it aside into a separate pile in their store. They asked us if it would be OK for them to smuggle this back across the front line to families who were trapped there and living in even more dire circumstances. These were people who chose to share their gifts immediately, despite their poverty, hardly letting them enter their possession before giving them away. A lesson in detachment perhaps – when we see things as undeserved gifts rather than possessions that we have a right to, they become a lot easier to give away.

I have on occasion seen the opposite attitude from those of great wealth who have worked all their lives to earn it. Sometimes, even when such people decide in principle to give some of it away, the process becomes a tortured one. Endless exercises in due diligence, needs assessments and the exact matching of projects with their particular interests can make it extremely difficult and sometimes impossible for them to give at the scale they had originally promised. There might be several factors at play here – including the sophistication and experience of people so successful in business – but one cause seems to be an understandably deep attachment to the wealth they have devoted so much of their life to accumulating. When they manage to give – and I know many of them who have found a way to do so remarkably freely – they deserve great respect, because they are very likely to feel a different sense of ownership of possessions earned by a lifetime of work compared to those who have, out of the blue been handed something from the back of a truck. And that is why developing that attitude of 'everything as gift' is crucial if we desire to become more charitable. Because the wealth accumulated by the 'self-made man' (what an absurd and revealing title), even if it appears otherwise, is no less a gift than the ones those refugees carried from the back of our lorry.

Our own mission of Mary's Meals tries to stay rooted in this attitude of 'sharing things that were never ours to keep'; a belief that the world's resources have been gifted for the benefit of everyone. We unashamedly proclaim our vision – that every child in this world might at least eat one meal every day in their place of education – because we know there is more than enough food in the world for this vision to become a reality. The only thing that needs to happen in order for it to be achieved is for an even greater number of those who have more than they need to be willing to share with those who do not even have enough food to eat.

Anyone, regardless of their faith or culture, can choose this approach (and the refugees in Zagreb were Muslim, by the way). But to follow Christ is to make charity our identity, our way of being. We can no longer be charitable on a part-time basis or apply that attitude to certain parts of our lives only. We cannot make distinctions between groups of people who might qualify for our charity based on race, or religion, or whether we like them, or whether we agree with them. When we dare to call ourselves Christians we say yes to a life of radical charity. We cannot be people who like to donate to faraway people who we have no personal relationship with, but meanwhile ignore our lonely housebound neighbour. Nor can we visit our housebound neighbour while ignoring the multitudes in faraway places who starve unnecessarily in this world of plenty. To be a Christian is to embrace an all-encompassing attitude of charity that will make demands on us every day. Anything else is a sham, a distortion of what it is to be Christian, an outrageous hypocrisy. But, sadly, that is what we Christians so often are; hypocrites not worthy of the name, often shown up by good people who do not share our faith, but who practise charity in a more impressive way. It wasn't always like this.

In AD 361, one generation after Emperor Constantine had first legalised Christianity in the Roman Empire, his nephew, Julian the Apostate, sought to restore paganism. On becoming Emperor, he set about trying to undermine the influence of 'the Galilean religion' in various ways, but he soon came to recognise the one great obstacle that was thwarting his ambitions of a pagan revival: Christian charity.

In a letter to a leading pagan high priest, he bemoaned: 'It is disgraceful that, when no Jew ever has to beg, and the impious Galileans [Christians] support not only their own poor but ours as well, all men see that our people lack aid from us.'

In their practice of charity, which they offered to all – not just adherents of their own religion – these 'Galileans' were demonstrating a charity that no pagan religion had ever stimulated. This was something new. While it was certainly building on the tenets of justice and love of neighbour inherited from Judaism, the teachings and actions of Christ turbocharged these moral imperatives and transformed them into a universal project that ultimately changed human society for ever. It is hard today to understand how revolutionary this was in a world that was then without any kind of social welfare, recognition of equality or concept of universal human rights. The full benefits to be gained from the Roman Empire were only available to a select group of Roman citizens. The multitudes of poor people, slaves and people from various other states and nations that made up the Empire – in fact the majority of people under Roman rule – did not share the same rights.

This startling new type of charity, based on the intrinsic value and dignity of every single person, was enormously attractive to many. That it would be imitated was inevitable. Emperor Julian's vigorous attempts to do so ultimately failed, despite him implementing the distribution of large quantities of grain and even wine in various parts of the Empire, including Galilee itself. Perhaps he failed because when a PR exercise masquerades as charity, sooner or later it will be found out. History tells us that Julian turned out to be the last pagan Roman Emperor. He couldn't compete with Christian charity – the radical startling new variety being practised by those crazy Galileans, who seemed only too willing to give everything away, even their own lives when persecutions came. Some of them in the early centuries chose to sell themselves into slavery so that the sum paid for them could be used as a ransom to set another free. Others chose voluntarily to go to prison to help those incarcerated there. This early Christian charity went some way beyond dropping a coin in the plate or buying a bacon roll at the parish coffee morning.

From the very beginning of Christianity, charity was recognised as one of its distinctive hallmarks and its earliest leaders, in their words and deeds, proclaimed it as essential and central for anyone wishing to follow Jesus. Even in the first few years immediately following Christ we learn from the Acts of the Apostles that works of charity blossomed among Christians so quickly that those apostles found it impossible to manage the administration created by these works alongside their other responsibilities. Very soon they appointed a new order of deacons, led by Stephen (soon to become their first martyr) and tasked them with this crucial mission.

Meanwhile, James, one of those apostles, was writing a letter to the Church, (now part of scripture) affirming the primacy of charity.

What good is it, my brothers, if someone says he has
faith but does not have works? Can that faith save him?
If a brother or sister is poorly clothed and lacking in
daily food, and one of you says to them, 'Go in peace, be
warmed and filled,' without giving them the things
needed for the body, what good is that? So, also faith by
itself, if it does not have works, is dead. (James 2:14–17,
ESV)

The following generations of bishops filled the early centuries
with calls to charity and justice, echoing the cries of the poor
over and over.

Irenaeus, Bishop of Lyon (AD 120–202), expanded on the
Old Testament teaching, in the new light of Christ, by
proclaiming the obligation of charity for all rather than to
select groups only:

Instead of the tithes, which the law commanded, the
Lord said to divide everything we have with the poor.
And he said to love not only our neighbours but also our
enemies, and to be givers and sharers not only with the
good but also to be liberal givers to those who take away
our possessions.

And St Gregory of Nazianzus (AD 329–389), Archbishop of
Constantinople, articulated with passion and beauty the
church's preferential love for the poor.

And if, following the command of Paul, and of Christ Himself, we suppose that love is the first and greatest of the commandments, the crowning point of the law and the prophets, I must conclude that love of the poor and compassion and sympathy for our own flesh and blood, is its most excellent form.

By the fourth century some of those fearless bishops had the rich – who were by now joining the Church in numbers for the first time – squirming in their seats. St John Chrysostom (AD 347–407), a later Archbishop of Constantinople, declared:

The rich are in possession of the goods of the poor, even if they have acquired them honestly or inherited them legally. Not to enable the poor to share in our goods is to steal from them and deprive them of life. The goods we possess are not ours but theirs.

And then he developed that theme in a way that perhaps feels even more pertinent today than it did sixteen hundred years ago.

All the wealth of the world belongs to you and to others in common, as the sun, air, earth and the rest. Do not say 'I am using what belongs to me.' You are using what belongs to others.

He was not one to mince his words!

It should not be surprising that the Church's charity and the call for justice have at times led to persecution, both by those striving to hold on to their privilege and those seeking revolution and popularity. There is significance in the fact that Saint Stephen, the first to be appointed to lead the Church's charity, became its first martyr, stoned to death while joyfully praising God. Those hungry for power, when they see the Church loving the poor, and the poor loving her, will sometimes even resort to violence.

St Basil of Caesarea (AD 330–379) used even more unsettling and dangerous rhetoric in his 'Sermon to the Rich', which he delivered as famine gripped his city and the suffering of the hungry was exacerbated by unscrupulous merchants holding back grain in order to increase prices.

> Which things, tell me, are yours? When have you
> brought your goods into life? You are like one occupying
> a place in a theatre who should prohibit others from
> entering, treating that as his own which is the common
> good of all. Such are the rich. If each would take that
> which is sufficient for his needs, leaving what is
> superfluous, to those in distress, no one would be rich or
> poor. The rich man is a thief.

But guidance on charity went well beyond giving the rich a hard time. The *way* in which the individual carried out charity was also of the utmost importance, as preached by St John Chrysostom again:

> Helping a person in need is good in itself. But the degree
> of goodness is hugely affected by the attitude with which
> it is done. If you show resentment because you are

helping the person out of a reluctant sense of duty, then the person may receive your help but may feel awkward and embarrassed. This is because he will feel beholden to you. If, on the other hand, you help the person in a spirit of joy, then the help will be received joyfully. The person will feel neither demeaned nor humiliated by your help, but rather will feel glad to have caused you pleasure by receiving your help. And joy is the appropriate attitude with which to help others because acts of generosity are a source of blessing to the giver as well as the receiver.

It's not difficult to see why his followers gave him the title 'Chrysostom', meaning 'golden mouth' in Greek.

And meanwhile the actions of some bishops were speaking even louder than their words. St Ambrose, Bishop of Milan (AD 339–397) once melted down some sacred vessels of his church in order to ransom captives. He defended this by saying 'the Church has gold not for keeping but for distributing and for aiding those in need'. And even from the first years after Christ we can see that the Church in some parts of the Empire began helping people in need even great distances away. St Cyprian, Bishop of Carthage, for example, sent a considerable sum of donations from his diocese in response to an appeal for help from the bishops of Numidia, which had been attacked by barbarians and where many people were left in urgent need of help. International aid began many centuries before the Industrial Revolution and the founding of the first 'humanitarian organisations'. It would serve us well when studying the history of charity and humanitarianism to broaden our history lessons and instead of considering only the past two hundred years, look instead at the last two thousand – and more. Otherwise, we are forsaking a treasure trove of wisdom that we need today more than ever.

The new religion of the Galileans was a radical one, practising what it preached and turning the world upside down. In a crumbling empire, awash with the destitute and hungry and without any type of social welfare, this Christian charity gave people new life and new meaning – both the givers and the receivers. Even attempted persecutions sometimes only succeeded in exposing this startling charity. During the early part of the fourth century the Romans raided a church in North Africa. They searched for treasure in the basement, as this is where they might have found it in a pagan temple. And there they did indeed find the treasure of that church, in the form of a well-stocked 'poor room' full of things donated for distribution to the needy. A surviving court record tells us that there were eighteen pairs of men's shoes, eighty-five pairs of women's shoes, thirteen dresses and ten vats of oil. That ancient inventory reminds me so much of the stock lists we used to write when we began collecting donations for our aid deliveries to Bosnia in the 1990s. Even the greater quantity of donated female garments compared to male has not changed! I can just imagine the men of that church in the fourth century discussing with their wives, as I did with Julie while packing our truck with gifts, whether that imbalance in donations was caused by the comparatively large size of women's hearts or their wardrobes?

I digress. And, unfortunately, so did the Church at times during some of the following centuries. In the Middle Ages charity was sometimes viewed as the sole preserve of the bishops, whose role it was to distribute donations, and whose practice of charity was mixed at best (not all of them lived up to the words and actions of their early predecessors), while the giving of alms by the ordinary person was sometimes primarily encouraged as a way to reduce their time in Purgatory. At times charity was considered more as a way of gaining preferential treatment on Judgement Day rather than a work of love, born out of compassion for the poor. Reform and renewal of charitable initiatives came at different times and in different shapes and sizes, often led by remarkable individuals such as St Francis of Assisi. With the Reformation, opinion about the role of good works in salvation became one of the contentious issues, the Protestants teaching that, while Christians should carry out good works, these were not essential to one's salvation because God's grace alone was enough, while Catholics maintained that we should participate in that salvation through the sacraments and through works of charity. Regardless of those differences, both Catholics and Protestants continued to generate all sorts of new charitable initiatives in the centuries after the reformation. One exceptional founder of new charitable initiatives was St Vincent de Paul, who came to prominence in the midst of another time of huge political change and enormous suffering caused by extreme poverty.

Having become a priest, it seems initially for reasons of ambition, during the early part of the seventeenth century Vincent found himself working in a French rural parish in which those without work sometimes starved to death. He began to develop a huge compassion for those he saw suffering there. One Sunday, as he was getting ready to celebrate

Mass, someone came into the sacristy to tell him of a destitute family in the parish who were all sick. There was no one to help them and they were completely without food and medicine. He entered the church and preached a sermon encouraging his parishioners to engage in works of charity, and told them of the family in their own parish in urgent need of help. That same Sunday evening he headed off to visit the family in distress and on the way, to his great amazement, came across a crowd of people that had heard him preach that morning making the same journey. That hot August evening the people processed as if on pilgrimage to the home of the sick family and delivered to them a huge pile of provisions. Once again charity was there, alive and well, in the hearts of those villagers ahead of any organisation, but Vincent recognised the need for that huge good will to be co-ordinated so that it could become effective. There was too much hunger in the land for a surplus of donated food to go to waste in the baking French summer. That family had more than they could possibly eat today, but tomorrow they would be hungry again.

Three days later Vincent held a meeting with some pious ladies of the parish and invited them to set up an association to provide ongoing support to the poor and sick of the parish. And thus began one of several missions founded by this man which grew to an astonishing size during his lifetime, and have grown even greater in the centuries since, while other organisations inspired by him and bearing his name have also had a huge impact on the world.

Nearly all churchgoing Catholics will know a parishioner who each Sunday stands at the exit of their church with a wooden collecting box soliciting funds in the name of St

Vincent de Paul in order to help the poorest in that parish and elsewhere. This society is known by different names in different parts of the world, but today has around 800,000 members in 140 different countries who take part in a simple practical works of charity as a way of living out their Christianity.

This is just one example among thousands of initiatives founded by devout Christians that have had a profound impact on the world. The list is endless: Martin Luther King and his crucial part in the struggle for civil rights, William Wilberforce's relentless fight to outlaw slavery, Florence Nightingale's founding of modern nursing, Elizabeth Fry's work in prisons, Desmond Tutu's championing of peace in South Africa, Mother Teresa's new army of nuns caring for the most destitute. And a vast array of Christian charities have been born to meet all sorts of human needs. Some, such as the Salvation Army and the YMCA, span the globe and are among the best known and most loved 'brands' in the world, while tens of thousands of small local initiatives are no less revered in the communities they serve. Vast international aid and development organisations have also grown out of various Christian denominations, including Christian Aid, World Vision, the Lutheran World Federation's World Service and the gargantuan network of Catholic Caritas organisations.

The example and teachings of the early church resonate through the ages, constantly finding new ways to express Christian charity in response to new needs and new possibilities. It seems that wherever Christianity is alive and well then so is charity. But the modern age is not without its challenges to both.

Despite all the evidence to the contrary, many in post-Christian Western Europe would not necessarily think of Christianity as a force for good in the world. Various scandals have undermined the credibility of the Church, which has also at times been portrayed as out of touch or viewed as being obsessed with certain ethical issues rather than the fundamental gospel message. Meanwhile, much of the Church in the West is in sharp decline and is struggling to know how to adapt to its loss of status and to finding itself once again on the periphery, no longer part of the establishment.

But it would be a big mistake for us modern-day Christians to feel sorry for ourselves. Those Christians of the early centuries faced much more daunting external foes than we do today. But they grew and flourished despite them, because their vibrant faith blossomed into wonderful acts of charity. 'See how they love each other!' exclaimed pagans unable to resist the wonder of it. And perhaps our newly diminished size and feelings of powerlessness are actually a beautiful opportunity to become more like those intrepid bands of early Christians; an opportunity to gaze upon the cross and remind ourselves that the one we serve chose to be broken and powerless too. But it isn't easy.

In the wealthy countries of the modern world it is perhaps harder to practise eye-catching, transformative acts of charity than it is in times and places of abject poverty, or in the absence of any type of social welfare. The early church, amid a multitude of hungry, enslaved, sick people, was almost starting with a blank canvas on which to write their good news in big bold letters. That sheet is now a beautiful and busy mosaic, and it would be hard to over-estimate the part that Christians over the past two thousand years have played in populating it. Who could claim to have performed a more important role in the founding of charities, schools, universities and hospitals? Who has done more to instil the concept of universal human rights, of equality, of the responsibility of governments to seek the common good rather than pursuing the privilege of a few? But in doing all these things and making the world so much better, in some parts of the developed world the Church has to an extent become a victim of its own success. Much of what it once pioneered and fought for is now taken for granted. Many of the gaps that their charity addressed are now filled by the state, or don't exist on the same scale because of the increased wealth in society and various advances in medicine and technology. There are few slave ships to liberate or lepers to kiss. In addition, a vast array of non-Christian charities have grown and flourished, performing all sort of crucial services. They play an enormous role in our civil society. Often they have imitated Christian charity, perhaps without even knowing it, and at least in part they are among its wonderful fruits.

But it would be absurd to assume that Christian charity is no longer required in the West. Needs have certainly changed – but perhaps not as much as we might think. Modern slavery is, sadly, alive and well in the form of human trafficking. The numbers of homeless people in our cities is an outrage. And while leprosy has long since been banished from Europe, there are new epidemics: drug addiction, obesity, self-harm, eating disorders – the list of modern plagues is a long and disturbing one. Children in the West very rarely suffer chronic malnutrition but often they are starved of a sense of identity and a sense of self-worth. And a sea of human misery means that currently every two hours a man in the UK takes his own life – suicide being the biggest killer of men under forty-five in the nation. Meanwhile, smaller family sizes and longer life expectancies are creating a demographic never seen before with enormous consequences. Caring for the elderly and loving the lonely are two enormous needs of our times, crying out for more charity.

Certain forms of charity might sometimes become redundant, or at least require a new approach, but charity itself never will. Needs shift. Society changes. The poor are to be found in different places and go by different names, but they are always with us, even in our own street or village. We will see them if we look hard enough.

And meanwhile, the poverty of our sisters and brothers in the world's poorest nations remains a scandal. There the most basic needs still go unmet on a vast scale. Each day, thousands of children are dying unnecessarily of causes related to hunger or from diseases that could be treated very easily and very cheaply. Huge injustices remain. The cry of the poor in sub-Saharan Africa, especially, is one we can hear clearly even on a blustery day in the far north of our planet.

And of course climate change, caused at least partly by those of us enjoying greedy lifestyles that the planet simply cannot sustain, is adding greatly to the suffering of those who were already the poorest. And we know that while that impact is, cruelly, being felt first and foremost by the world's poorest communities, it won't be long before it diminishes the quality of the life of our children and our children's children. A whole range of new charitable activities aimed at addressing this –

both to meet the needs of those already affected and to tackle the root causes – are urgently needed.

It is clear then, that there is no shortage of charitable work needing to be done. And there never will be, as long as human beings inhabit the Earth. Christian charity continues to lead the way in many areas of greatest need in the world's poorest nations. So many depend on it for life, for healthcare, for schools and for support in their struggle against injustice and oppression. In the face of this century's new horror – the colossal HIV/AIDS epidemic, which has devastated the lives of tens of millions in the developing world – the Church has once again been at the forefront of the charitable response. It is estimated that, globally, 25 per cent of victims of the disease are receiving care and treatment from the Catholic Church alone.

It can be no coincidence that the Church continues to grow and be most vibrant in the world's poorest places. Here the joy of the gospel and its radical living of the message of love are hard to ignore or resist.

In the West it can feel very different. As Christians we need to find ways to be become more joyful and more radical in our practice of charity. Perhaps we need to look to our forefathers and mothers in faith, whose zeal in living the gospel prompted works of love so beautiful they won over an empire. For the health of the Church and the vibrancy of its charity will always be inextricably linked – one is a barometer of the other.

9

Transformation

And remember, the truth that once was spoken:
to love another person is to see the face of God.

VICTOR HUGO, *LES MISÉRABLES*

Claudio, an elderly Italian gentleman, lived in the south of England and was housebound. His carers were the only people who called at his door most weeks, although someone in his parish visited occasionally. He left his house only for hospital appointments which, as a result of his failing health, were becoming more frequent.

A nun who called in to see him was the first to tell him about Mary's Meals. Claudio loved children and delighted in the thought of being able to help some of the poorest in the world. He began to give the carers his bank card to get out some cash which he would then post to us, always in a padded envelope with 'Document Enclosed' written on it in beautiful, distinctive handwriting. These began to arrive every month at our office, always accompanied by a warm, carefully written letter. Occasionally he missed a month and the next donation would then be double the size to make up for it, accompanied by a letter explaining that he had been in hospital and unable to post his usual gift.

He began to call the office quite frequently, initially to let us know to expect an envelope from him, then to check it had arrived, then yet again to thank us for the thank-you letter we had sent him. Beautifully written letters always accompanied each donation. He began to tell us more about himself – mainly about his poor health and isolation. His phone calls got longer. Everyone in our office, including my wife Julie, loved to hear from Claudio and understood that listening to him was as important as the gift he was giving. He said he felt part of Mary's Meals, as if it was a family to him.

Then Claudio began to get a little confused, not remembering when he had sent his last donation and sometimes getting frustrated with us if we had sent him a letter he didn't want, or conversely, if we didn't send him one he did want.

One day Julie answered Claudio's call and he sounded unhappy. She chatted with him for some time but remained unsure that he had really understood what she had tried to explain. She decided to post him a copy of my book, *The Shed That Fed a Million Children*, along with a little note. A couple of days later she got a phone call from a very joyful Claudio, who explained he had already read the book from cover to cover. He said he absolutely loved it and everything about Mary's Meals. Best of all, he said he now understood everything. He was particularly delighted to learn that the Julie who he had been speaking with so often and already made friends with, was my wife. From then on, whenever he called the office he always asked for Julie. He would call us his 'dear friends' and tell us he loved us all. In fact, in every letter and during every phone call, he never failed to tell us how much he loved us.

He said some beautiful things about Mary's Meals – that he knew he was part of the Mary's Meals family and that it gave him great joy to know that he was able to help children even though his health was failing and he was housebound. He said that Mary's Meals made him a better person, that it made him happy, that it gave him purpose. Once he said Mary's Meals was 'like Eucharist to the hungry child'. He said Mary's Meals would be with him until the very end.

One day when he became more ill Julie asked our younger children to make him a get well card. He loved that card too. He said that during the nights when the pain kept him awake he liked to look at the card and that it brought him joy. He reciprocated by sending his carers out to the shops to buy chocolates to send our children.

It was obvious by now that his health was failing more dramatically. His letters were muddled and his phone calls sporadic. One afternoon he called the office sounding very weak. He explained he was waiting for the ambulance to take him to hospital, so he thought he would phone us in the meantime. He talked and talked. He was sad and tired but kept telling Julie, 'I love you very much,' and she would reply, 'we love you too, Claudio.' Everyone in our little office felt sad at the end of that call and concerned at how poorly Claudio had sounded.

A few days later his neighbour called to tell us that Claudio had been diagnosed with leukaemia. He said he phoned because Claudio talked about us all the time and loved Mary's

Meals more than anything. The next morning, the neighbour called again. Claudio had passed away overnight. In the office they cried a little, and prayed, and talked about Claudio and his love for Mary's Meals. We asked our parish priest to offer Holy Mass for him and sent the little Mass card to his friends care of his home address, in the hope that they might realise that we too loved Claudio.

The following Sunday my mum delivered Julie and I a letter that had arrived at her house by mistake. Julie immediately recognised the distinctive handwriting as Claudio's. 'My very dear friends, if you are reading this then it means Our Good and Loving Lord has called me home to heaven ...' He continued to say some very beautiful things about Mary's Meals and what we all meant to him, and he ended the letter, as he ended every letter and every phone call, with 'I love you very much.'

When Julie added up all the gifts he had so faithfully and lovingly sent in the three years that had known about Mary's Meals, she realised that the 'little acts of love' he had made from his housebound existence were enough to feed 117 children. The lives of those children will have been changed by him. But his own life had been changed at least as much by his choice to give in the way he did.

Although we never met Claudio, to be able to journey with him was a gift in a number of ways. The encounter provided us with new insights into the depth and beauty of charity. When someone practises authentic charity things start to change – not only for the one they are helping, and not only for themselves, but for others involved in the process – and even for a wider circle of people who might start to see new dim shapes made visible by the faint distant light cast by a little candle held by someone like Claudio.

Sometimes these changes happen immediately. At other times it takes longer – years, decades, generations even. But change always happens. Some of the fruits of our labour become ripe only after many years, requiring whole trees to grow first, while others bloom almost instantaneously in the desert before our very eyes. The children that Claudio helped would have begun to experience change very quickly indeed.

In the sorts of schools that they attend, playgrounds are too often misnomers; places where children don't play. And lunch breaks are all too often times when children don't eat. Instead, they sit silently in the shade of their classroom wall or perhaps sleep beneath the merciful branches of a thorny old tree. Quiet playgrounds are sad places. A very dramatic transformation occurs in those situations when a school meal is served and breaks their long fast. Stomach pains begin to fade and energy stirs even as they clean the last morsel from their plates. The silence gives way to chatter and then laughter and before long the children are playing in the dust. Food makes things better very quickly for a hungry child.

The donation of such a meal has an immediate obvious impact; an easy thing to anticipate and explain and report on. And the very first time such meals are served in a particular school is normally a day of exuberant celebration, when the community (which may, based on previous experiences, have had reason to doubt whether the 'talk' would really translate into a meaningful reality) expresses its joy. It can feel as if hope has just entered in and the community sing and dance to welcome it. Such a day will have been preceded by community meetings, volunteer training, the construction of kitchens and the solving of logistical challenges (the food might have been delivered by trucks, donkeys, dug-out canoes or even on the heads of willing, strong people – the modes of transport vary wildly).

On one such occasion the headteacher of a school in Haiti described the anticipation and reaction of his school community.

'The first day with meals the students were happy! One even said, as they waited, "Once the food is actually in my mouth. I will believe it." And when the food was served one of them said "Is this really me sitting here eating? Am I not in a dream?"'

A beaming mother of a child at that same school spoke of her son's reaction on his return home that first day.

'They gave me lots of food, Mum!' he exclaimed to her.

The difference between a school day without food and one with a generous serving of rice and beans is a vast one that prompts instantaneous elation – not just for the child but for the parent too. For the anguish caused by not being able to feed your own child is an awful one – at least as terrible as the hunger itself.

That headteacher described with glee how, almost immediately, children who had been out of school began coming back because of the promise of a meal. In fact, often we see enrolment in a school rise significantly even before the serving of our first meals – the promise that the meals will appear being incentive enough for some parents to send children from their place of work to the classroom.

When our giving causes such instantaneous and dramatic results it can be immediately gratifying. The familiar question of 'will it make a difference?' is answered before it even has a chance to form properly.

I am sure that some of the benefits in Claudio's life – and in many donors' lives – were and are immediate also. We tend to feel a little stab of joy when we share something; and the idea of a hungry child now eating because of our gift makes us happy. But some of the more profound changes take longer to appear for the giver and the receiver too. And some of them are all the more wonderful because they were not foreseen.

In Chapter 3 I wrote about Yamakani, the orphan girl looking after her younger brothers on her own in Malawi during a year of famine. It was clear when I met them that the guarantee of our daily meal was vital to their survival. A couple of years later I received the startling news that Yamakani had done so well in her final primary school exams that she had been offered an extremely rare, and enormously precious, free place in secondary school. Suddenly her life prospects had shifted dramatically. All sorts of things were now possible. For this Yamakani herself deserves the credit. She achieved those outstanding grades while trying to fend for her little brothers each day. I remember her describing to me how they struggled with their homework because they did not have any kind of light at home which would allow them to read after dusk. I really do not know how she did it, but I do know that without the gift of a meal each day, made by some faraway donor, she would not have been able to do so.

Outcomes like this cannot be predicted with any certainty. Our gifts are often a small part in the large tapestry of someone's life. A lot of the time we are only the planter of little seeds, or the hired hands that weed the fields; maybe we have the joy of being there at harvest time. But none of us has responsibility for it all or can take credit for what happens in someone else's life. Sometimes we can see that our charitable acts have indeed played a vital part, and one perhaps that can only be seen when we look back over a longer span of years.

In January 2002 a little group of orphans in Chilomoni – a ramshackle township on the edge of Blantyre, Malawi – queued up for the very first Mary's Meals ever served in a place of education. Among them was a little girl called Veronica. I don't remember her then as an individual, but I do recall clearly that little group of children, the poorest of the poor in their community, who in the absence of parents were being cared for by grandmothers, aunts, uncles and older siblings.

It was only much later that I came to know Veronica. We were making a documentary about young people who had benefited from Mary's Meals and our team in Malawi told me of this amazing young lady called Veronica who, like Yamakani, had progressed through primary school with the help of our daily meals and secured a chance to go to secondary school. Then, even more incredibly, she had been offered a place at university. While we filmed with her at Blantyre Polytechnic we learnt more about her story: she was an orphan raised by her older sisters, and when she was very young they sometimes went for as long as a week without food at home. She only started going to school because of the promise of food there. We were astounded to learn that she had been among that very first group of children to benefit from our meals in Chilomoni.

While I have been writing this book, Veronica has graduated from university with a degree in Education. She is a confident, articulate young woman who is determined to play her part in bringing about change in Malawi. Her remarkable journey has been made possible first of all by her own strength and talent, but it has also been made possible by various acts of charity, including the meals provided by faraway strangers.

Please God, Veronica – and others of her generation – will bring about change in their nation that will mean that students will no longer depend on the charity of strangers in order to gain an education, and growing children might take for granted that their daily need for food will be met by their own families and communities. Armed with their education and health, Veronica and her peers can play their part in bringing about political change, economic growth and the eradication of endemic corruption. But for now, it can be seen that charity played its part – a crucial part – in bringing that day closer. Lots of little acts of love are transforming the lives of strangers and of society more generally.

The story I told of that little deaf boy in Liberia who the police had dropped at the door of our new Oscar Romero School for the Deaf has also developed in a beautiful way. Having learnt in the years since how to communicate with sign language and having gained an education, Joseph and a fellow student from the school have both been offered places at college. They are the first ever children from a school for the deaf in Liberia to receive such offers. This is a truly wonderful and significant victory in the lives of those young people, but also in the story of Liberia – a nation struggling with all its might to recover from war and escape poverty.

Charitable organisations have a strong desire to try to
capture evidence of the kind of change seen in the lives of
Yamakani, Veronica and Joseph and link it to their own
endeavours. In order to understand whether their efforts are
efficient and effective, they must find ways to monitor and
evaluate their work and its impact. Part of this process will
often be to define a 'theory of change' that identifies various
hoped-for outcomes that will be achieved by their work, along
with a way to measure these. If evidence can be found that
such outcomes are happening, the theory will be proven
correct. Such exercises can also reveal that the results are not
what was expected or hoped for, therefore allowing this
learning to inform changes to the model. A 'theory of change'
can therefore be crucial to organisations that constantly wish
to learn and to improve what they are doing, and are also
essential in demonstrating to certain types of funders that the
desired impact is indeed being achieved. They can be a very
important tool – a great example of the role the head should
play in the work of charity. However, such efforts are limited.
The crucial role our heart plays is a much harder thing to
depict in a flow chart or represent in a spreadsheet. The
sometimes subtle, hard-to-define changes that take place in
people can be impossible to quantify. It is very important to
recognise that; otherwise, before you know it, things that
cannot be captured by a 'theory of change' are deemed
worthless or irrelevant. And those things might just be the
most important of all.

'Intense love doesn't measure, it just gives,' Mother Teresa
once said – and that was an appropriate thing for her to say
about the distinct approach undertaken by her Missionaries

of Charity. For most who organise charity, though, certain things should to be measured as we exercise our responsibility as stewards of the gifts of others and our desire to become better at what we do – as long as we remember that we cannot capture everything that is important in this way. The kind of change that can occur in the life of the giver is often especially hard to calculate. In the life of Claudio, for example, things became better because of his giving. He was not suddenly relieved of his physical suffering, but over a period of time he seemed to find a new joy in his feeling of belonging to something and a new sense of purpose and meaning. He appeared to have become a man at peace with himself and the world by the end of his life – and his charity had played a key part in that.

Our lives too were touched by our encounter with Claudio. Certainly some of the joy he experienced was also shared by us. Our lives were enriched when we realised that this rather sad and isolated man was becoming happier and less lonely though his interactions with us. Our daily work was given more meaning when we saw how enabling someone to participate in our mission could create such a happy transformation. His acts of charity certainly brought about the kind of change we would expect and hope for in the lives of hungry children, but they did much more than that.

There was also a spiritual element that ran through our encounters with Claudio. He made increasingly frequent references to his own faith during his communications with us. He even made that arresting comment about Mary's Meals being 'like Eucharist to the hungry child'. I am not sure if this observation was prompted by him simply thinking about the correlation between the physically hungry child being fed our meals and the spiritually hungry person being fed by the Eucharist (Holy Communion), or whether it was a more fundamental notion that acts of charity are, in a sense, also sacramental in nature. But either way, he was pointing to very ancient wisdom indeed.

Several hundred years before Christ, in the book of Deuteronomy, the fifth book of the Old Testament, also known as *Devarim* in the Jewish Torah, precise guidelines on tithing were set out. According to a prescribed, seven-year cycle, certain portions of produce were to be offered to the temple each year. In some years some of these tithes were to be distributed to the poor. In this way, gifts to those in need were considered 'sacred offerings' – they were being given to God, as well as to the people in need of them.

In the same way, in the early Christian church, there was a central belief that giving to the poor was a direct way to encounter God. The passage in Matthew's Gospel in which Jesus taught that by feeding the hungry we are feeding Him, or that by carrying out other acts of mercy we are being merciful to Him was not treated as a metaphor. It was taken very literally indeed. In the poor person God Himself could be encountered.

The famous story of Saint Martin of Tours demonstrates this in a memorable way. Martin, who was eventually to become the patron saint of France, where today over 4,000 churches are named after him, was born in present-day Hungary in around AD 315. Although his parents were both pagans, Martin decided he wanted to be a Christian at the age of ten and became a catechumen (one who is being prepared for baptism). As his father was a soldier in the Roman Army, Martin was obliged to follow in his father's footsteps and ended up spending five years in the imperial cavalry. It was while he was posted in northern Gaul, where his troops were fighting the Franks, that a celebrated incident occurred. While on garrison duty in Amiens, on a bitterly cold winter's night, Martin rode out through the city gate. There he noticed a pitifully dressed beggar who looked at risk of freezing to death. Martin removed his large white cloak – part of the standard garb of Roman lancers – and used his sword to cut it in half. Giving one half to the beggar, he rode on wearing the remaining half himself.

That same night Martin had a dream in which Jesus appeared to him wearing the part of the cloak he had given to the beggar, saying, 'Martin, still a catechumen, covered me with his cloak.'

His dream echoed those words of Jesus, recorded by Matthew: 'For I was lacking clothes and you clothed me.' (Matthew 25:36, NJB) And this concept became connected in a particular way to the celebration of the Eucharist. Just a few decades after Martin's encounter with the beggar, our friend with the 'golden mouth', St John Chrysostom, kissed the altar in his Church at Antioch, as a priest always does before celebrating Holy Mass. Some minutes later, in his sermon, he acknowledged the respect his congregation showed for the altar on which the Mass was being celebrated. He pointed out that they venerated it both because it received the Body of Christ, and because it was an image of Christ Himself, before suggesting that the one in the church wasn't the only 'altar' in Antioch.

'Whenever you see a poor believer, imagine that you behold an altar. Whenever you meet a beggar, don't insult him but reverence him,' he said. The Eucharist being celebrated on the altar and the poor person being ministered to on the street; both were to be revered as ways of meeting the living Lord.

The celebration of that Mass in Antioch then continued with the offertory, when the gifts of bread and wine to be consecrated would have been presented to the priest while at the same time a collection of money for the poor and the upkeep of the church would have been taken up from the congregation and brought to the altar too. The invitation to drop coins or notes into a basket or plate each Sunday is perhaps, for a lot of us, the earliest childhood opportunity we were given to make a donation. But for many of us – and I certainly include myself in this – this can become a routine activity that doesn't feel much like an act of charity. In my case it can often become a frantic exploration of – hopefully not empty – pockets, and the gift becomes just whatever might happen to be lurking there.

Attending celebrations of the Mass in Liberia during their civil war helped me think about this part of the service in a new way. In those little villages, where the people were nearly all subsistence farmers engaged in a relentless struggle to survive, there was at that time almost no money in circulation. The gifts collected for the church and poor could only be in the form of their own produce, and so instead of passing round a basket or plate, the parishioners danced up the aisle carrying pineapples, bunches of plantain and even a few live chickens and laid them in front of the altar. Afterwards, these precious gifts were gathered into Father Garry's old pick-up truck and driven to the next village, where, before Mass was celebrated there, they would be given to the elders for distribution to the most destitute in their community. And then the same thing would happen at the Mass in that village and once again, afterwards, the pick-up would be refilled with colourful vegetables and squawking chickens. Then they would go on to yet another village where the process would be repeated yet again. Sometimes Father Garry and his co-workers would take some fruit, or occasionally even roast one of the chickens for their Sunday dinner – this being the part offered for 'the church' – but this was in essence a merry-go-round that enabled each village to share something with the poorest of the poor in the neighbouring one. This experience brought alive for me certain aspects of the Mass – especially the centrality of 'charity' in Eucharistic celebration. It helped me also to think afresh about the 'universal destination of goods': the idea that everything has been given us as a gift and should be shared and used by us for the good of all, and that we should thank God for it.

At those Masses in the Liberian bush, and in Antioch 1,700 years earlier, the priest prayed over the bread offered saying:

> Blessed are you Lord, God of all creation. Through your goodness we have this bread to offer, which earth has given and human hands have made. It will become for us the bread of life.

When Claudio pointed to our work of charity being somehow Eucharistic, he was perhaps echoing this profession of thanks to a good God who has created everything we could ever have or benefit from. Anything we are able to offer back – whether it be a crumpled £10 note or a flapping chicken – must have first of all been a gift to us. We are taking part in a celebration through which the 'bread that belongs to all' is redistributed accordingly, making that truth a reality. The opportunity to give alms during Mass allows us to worship God in a special way. Our act of giving is transformed and becomes also something sacred: something that enriches this encounter – this Communion – between us and God, and between us and our brothers and sisters.

And this giving allows us to reflect on something else too. The Eucharistic celebration is a memorial of the death and resurrection of Jesus. Later in that same prayer, the priest of the early church, the priest of today and the thousands in the centuries in between, will proclaim the death and resurrection of Jesus, along with his congregation: 'We proclaim your death, O Lord, and profess your resurrection until you come again.' The people gathered believe they are acting out the greatest ever act of mercy. In sharing a little of what they have during that ceremony, they are finding another way to participate in it. This is just one reason why the Mass is in fact not just an acting out but something new each time – and something participatory.

But it is not only participation in the Mass that affords this possibility. Every sincere act of charity, if we wish it to, reflects this central event of the Christian faith – that perfect act of charity that we have benefited from. And regardless of our own particular faith tradition, every freely given gift we make might acknowledge God as the creator of all things – the one who gave freely to us first of all. And each little act of love we make might point again to a God of tenderness and mercy, as He is described by the psalmist and numerous times elsewhere in Scripture.

When we participate in works of charity, regardless of the scale of our giving and our own particular faith tradition, or whether we ever attend Eucharistic celebrations, we may be doing something much more momentous than performing the immediate practical act. We may in fact be revealing something about the nature of God and the world He created. It might be that each time we perform authentic charity we create a deeper, more broadly shared understanding of ourselves and the world we live in. Each time we light one of our little candles in the gloom we illuminate a little more the most fundamental truths of our existence. We challenge assumptions that the most important currencies of this world are money or personal success, and instead reveal more fully the kind of world this could be: the kind of world its creator intended it to be, a world ruled by a different economy – an economy of compassion, mercy and love.

I think believers and non-believers alike share the hope that human goodness proclaims something deeper about our universe: a desire, perhaps unconscious, that goodness wins out in the end, that those who strive for what is right might somehow be satisfied, and that the world and its future might be shaped by such goodness in more profound ways than the immediate measurable outcomes of our endeavours.

Perhaps this is starting to sound a bit lofty. I don't think Claudio would have made such audacious claims about the potential of his modest gifts to change the world. And I certainly take a risk in straying into theological discussion well beyond my qualifications. But I cannot but try to express something I feel each time I witness remarkable practitioners of charity act. Such people are servants of hope. When I watch them I certainly feel new hope rise in me. And I see it rising in others too – a burning hope that things will get better, that even if the candles are few and tiny, they will always overcome the darkness, that somehow the laws of the universe have been written in such a way that the last candle cannot ever be extinguished and that we, as carriers of the light, cannot – ultimately at least – be defeated, that the apostles of love win in the end. Charity shouts these things loudly, even when done quietly – perhaps especially when it is done quietly.

It seems to me that questions about charity being naïve, unnecessary, outdated or perhaps incapable of tacking the underlying causes of poverty, can in fact be turned upside down. If we desire human development and the creation of a better world for all, we surely must have sight of a broader spectrum of life than the utilitarian goals of humanitarianism and international development. Those goals are very good, but they are not enough on their own. It is not charity that is limited in its ambition, but more often those who accuse it of such. If we believe that every answer to human suffering is to be found in economic growth we are hopelessly naïve. If we think the kind of charity practised by the early Christians, and by many others with huge hearts before them and since, is obsolete, we can only be deaf to the cries of so many who suffer around us even in the midst of wealth never seen before in the history of the world. And if we feel that a charity of love and faith is outdated, we disdain the wisdom of our ancestors, on which our own civilisation – at least the very best bits of it – were founded.

But that accusation of this type of charity not being able to tackle the underlying causes of poverty? Perhaps that one holds a bit more weight. The people in the church listening to St John Chrysostom, like everyone else in the pre-modern era, could never have entertained a serious conversation about solving world poverty, or set about creating a plan to eradicate global hunger. The advances in technology and the lessons of history show us that humanity can indeed sometimes make massive strides forward and overcome certain sources of suffering: that we can think bigger than just meeting the immediate need, that we do not have to accept that our streets are full of beggars but instead create systems of social care that help prevent that eventuality. The eradication of a disease like smallpox – and soon leprosy and polio – are fine examples of what can be achieved by clever, determined and good human beings.

And yet today over 100 million school-age children are chronically hungry. Many thousands of them will have died today of hunger-related causes, despite the fact that we know the cure for hunger. In this battle we are not waiting for some medical or scientific breakthrough. Yes, it is important that we continue to develop our agricultural methods to grow better, cheaper food for future generations as our populations grow, and yes, it is chronic poverty that ultimately causes such hunger, but the fact is that today while many children starve, we live in a world that already produces more than enough food for all – easily. Those children suffer today through a shortage of love rather than a shortage of food. And all those people suffering chronic loneliness? We know the cure for that one too. And while huge improvements have been made since the days of the Roman Empire, the briefest walk in most city centres will remind us that begging has not yet been consigned to history. But it could be if our society and policy-makers were more profoundly charitable.

Basic charity is needed now as much as ever. It does not always have to be the sort that makes bold claims about trans- forming the world. Sometimes the best sort is happy to leave that to others and, indeed, rejoices in those who more dramat- ically tear down walls of injustice while it continues quietly with its tiny unsung little acts of love. For through those seemingly insignificant, unrecorded deeds, our universe is in fact changed irreversibly. It is not necessary for us to think that way every time we make an online donation or run 5 kilometres with a charity T-shirt on, but it is important that we do not allow our little gifts to be demeaned as being irrel- evant or naïve. Charity that enables people to understand more fully the wonder of themselves and the wonder of the world is a much more ambitious project than any of those aimed at economic development or the eradication of a disease.

Acts of charity allow light to enter the world – including the ends of the spectrum not visible to the human eye. The most wondrous consequences of charity are not always conspicuous or easy to quantify but that should not lead us to make the catastrophic mistake of thinking those things are less important.

Claudio did not just feed 117 children.

10

Charity Remains

As it is, these remain: faith, hope and love, the three
of them; and the greatest of them is love.

1 CORINTHIANS 13:13

'It all sounds great, but is it really sustainable?' asked the earnest
young man in the midst of the debate I was having with an
enthusiastic audience of MBA students in Barcelona. To be
truthful, at that point I was getting slightly irked by the question. I had heard it repeated frequently and was always unsure,
initially, exactly what the poser of the question meant – and on
probing I sometimes discovered that they didn't either. When
asked by someone from a grantmaking body, such as a government department, it seemed most often to mean 'What is your
exit strategy? When can you hand this over to the government
of the country you are working in?' These are important and
valid questions, but I am not sure a project handed over to a
government is necessarily a sustainable one. I have seen good
projects fail too often, after such a handover, to accept that this
step in itself, makes something sustainable.

That particular MBA student, it seemed, through further conversation, was thinking mainly about economic sustainability. If we continued to add more and more schools to our feeding programme, how could this be funded into the future? This was a sensible question.

Increasingly, that same question has more often been focused on environmental matters. Is our work being done in a way that contributes to global warming? What kind of fuel are we using? Do we have to make so many flights? These are more good questions about an enormously important topic – so important, in fact, that in 2015 the UN replaced its Millennium Development Goals with Sustainable Development Goals; these being the agreed seventeen priorities of the international community when working on the progress of humanity.

The goals are generally laudable. I especially like the first two which cannot be criticised as lacking in ambition:

1. End Poverty in All its Forms
2. Zero Hunger

And their definition of sustainable development is clear: 'development that meets the needs of the present without compromising the ability of future generations to meet their own needs'.

On reading this extensive charter, though, I am left with a mixture of feelings. On one hand, it is uplifting to see the international community sign up to a shared vision on such an array of issues and pledge their efforts to collaborate on these. But there is another part of me that is left feeling that the most important parts of humanity, the things that would give me most hope for our collective future, are missing. The heart is missing. The head has become a lone operative. The spiritual dimension of humankind is absent. I understand why that is the case – this a UN charter, not poetry, or a Papal Encyclical. The UN has its own important role in the world and that is fine, as long as we do not forget the parameters which limit it. When its website states that 'The 2030 Agenda for Sustainable Development provides a global blueprint for dignity, peace and prosperity for people and the planet, now and in the future,' it might be wise for us to remember that its observations about 'dignity, peace and prosperity' are greatly constrained in their depth and breadth, as is any vision it might hold for our future and how that future might best come about. Charity, faith, hope, joy and beauty are words that cannot find their way into a document like that, and yet, if we are interested in sustainability and the future of our race, these are the things that ultimately endure, the things which inspire us to want a better, more fully human future for all in the first place, and the things that can provide us with optimism that this can be so.

Surely the development of humanity needs a holistic approach, one which includes the finest attribute of humanity, the thing we can be most proud of: charity? And charity is certainly sustainable. In fact, it is more than sustainable – much more. For it does not operate in the currency of finite things. The kind of light that charity allows to enter in is not generated by an energy source that can ever become depleted. The more we let in, the more there is, shining ever more brightly, even in the blackest night. That kind of light does not need to be conserved. And not only that – charity begets charity in all sorts of ways.

Katarina Zarinkijević was born in February 1991 in Vukovar, a city lying on the banks of the River Vuka, which divides Croatia from Serbia. This was not a great place to be born at that point in history. By then Yugoslavia was already starting to tear apart, and during the second half of the year of her birth, Vukovar suffered an eighty-seven-day siege. During that time, as many as 12,000 rockets and shells were being fired at the city each day. Vukovar has been described as the first European city to be completely destroyed by human conflict since the Second World War.

During this horror Katarina and her family fled west to Slavonski Brod, another town lying on a river border (this time the Sava, which divides Croatia from Bosnia–Herzegovina). It too was soon being fired on from across the water, but compared to Vukovar it was safe and so they stayed there along with thousands of other displaced people. They were all very dependent on humanitarian aid.

I came to know Slavonski Brod quite well during those years. Julie, my future wife, and I often drove there along back roads and dirt tracks (the highways having been rendered impassable by the fighting) in order to deliver truck-loads of gifts from Scotland. I remember the snapped bridges across the river and the hasty barricades erected along the riverbank to provide some kind of protection from the snipers' bullets. I remember, too, the crowds of people who would queue patiently at the back of our truck as we opened it and began to distribute food and other basic items to those in need. We employed a very primitive method of rationing, with each person being encouraged by our local partner organisation, The Family Centre, to arrive with one empty carrier bag in which the foodstuffs for each family were carried away.

Katarina was very small then, and today has only hazy recollections of that part of her life. But she remembers the trucks of food and other supplies arriving (perhaps ours among them), and in particular she remembers being given a blanket that filled her with delight. It felt so soft and smelt so new – a gift from someone she never knew in a faraway place.

Today Katerina lives in Zagreb, the capital of Croatia, and works as a teacher in a nursery school. Much of her time outside of work is spent volunteering for Mary's Meals, organising various fundraising events including a costume ball and an annual 5-kilometre run through a city park, in which thousands of people participate. Katarina is not alone in this mission – anything but. A remarkable and vibrant volunteer movement in support of Mary's Meals has flourished in Croatia and Bosnia–Herzegovina – perhaps partly because of the history of our organisation, within which Katarina's story is far from unique. Many involved here in this mission to help feed children in faraway countries were once the recipients of such help themselves. In fact Mary's Meals Croatia was founded by the friends we worked with at The Family Centre during the war, who I remember even then saying to us, 'one day, when things are better for us here, we want to do this too – help people in other countries'. They have kept that promise in a spectacular way. Their fundraising efforts in Croatia are relentless and are enabling tens of thousands of children to eat at school in the developing world. This is a relatively new way of expressing charity in Croatia, so our old friends there are also instrumental in creating cultural change in their country. Katerina says:

> Maybe this experience from my childhood is one of the reasons I decided to join the Mary's Meals family and help raise awareness about how little is needed to change the life of one child in a distant country. Growing up, I was always included in volunteering but when I decided that I wanted to give more, Mary's Meals found their way to my heart. I feel that now I can return the help my people, my family and I once got from someone who did not know us. I guess I want to pay it forward.
>
> When I give my time or talent to help spread the word about Mary's meals I feel like I am giving one child a chance to make it through life. Like I once got. Because not one child should be denied a happy and carefree childhood. This makes me rethink my life and how happy I am that I am alive and independent today. I can only be grateful to God for everything I have and be His voice and helping hand for His children in need.'

When Mrs Marihart sent me that second package from Innsbruck containing news that she had now raised the funds to feed 1,000 children (with all those stories of her fundraising efforts in her school), she told me something else in her letter too.

Oh, how happy my kids from school were (especially class 2a) when they watched the video!!! And then they said 'Let's go on! Let's get some more Mary's Meals kids!'

And at the end of the school year (my last as a teacher, I am retired now) they asked me 'Hey, Miss Marihart, who will do Mary's Meals next year when you are retired?' As I sadly shrugged my shoulders and said, 'I really don't know because this means work and responsibility and I cannot pull over my work to another teacher', then four or five of my pupils shouted 'We will do it! Can't we do it? Oh what a shame – we want to continue!!'

And so Magnus there is a class in a little village nearby Innsbruck who will continue. They arc about 13 years now. I do not know how long their fire for Mary's Meals will burn. But a seed is put into the ground of their hearts and souls, a seed of humanity and taking care of others. Probably the seed was there before and we just helped the little plant to grow.

But life, as we know, doesn't consist only of stories with happy endings. I suppose if it were so charity would find itself redundant. The problem of pain will forever accompany us on our journeys. The mystery of suffering remains. And suffering and charity will always be found in the same sorts of places, just in the way that close to each patch of nettles you can invariably find some dock leaves (the ones that heal the stings of nettles). They grow there quietly, unnoticed, until we urgently look for them to ease our pain – or the pain of someone else.

Claudio was a man who in his own pain found a way to give of himself. His intention to begin with was simply to help some hungry children in Africa. In so doing he found a new sense of meaning and created new relationships, including one with us that, with the receipt of his posthumous letter, lasted beyond death. In a sense he built a memorial for himself out of acts of charity.

A young boy called Charlie Craig from County Down, in Northern Ireland, lived a story much more painful to recount. He was diagnosed with leukaemia when he was only two years of age and began intensive therapy, including two bone marrow transplants. We first heard of Charlie when he donated all the money he had been given for his First Communion to Mary's Meals. But he didn't stop there. Despite his devastating illness, he not only continued fundraising for our cause, but for various other charities too. For example, he painted beautiful stones and sold them to raise money. But his suffering increased when he developed a chronic complication related to the bone marrow transplants. Eventually he died at nine years old, having already learnt more about giving and receiving charity than most of us do during much longer lives.

I learnt of Charlie's death just as I was about to give a talk about Mary's Meals at Mladifest, the huge annual international youth festival at Medjugorje, and was therefore able to ask the tens of thousands present to pray for his devastated family. Receiving the news there made me think about my own brother Mark.

He, too, died before his time, although he had much longer on this Earth than little Charlie. But like Charlie, his serious and painful illness didn't deter him from works of charity. And in fact it was during a previous Mladifest in Medjugorje that he died, at thirty-nine years of age. He had asked to accompany me there so that he could help distribute Mary's Meals leaflets and talk to those who wanted to volunteer. His whole life had been marred by chronic pain caused by a skin disease for which the doctors could find no cure. It caused him terrible physical suffering but also emotional and psychological pain. It was a disease that disfigured him in ways that led strangers to stare and children who didn't know him to sometimes visibly recoil. Not the children who knew him though – he was my own children's favourite uncle. They loved his company because he loved them and delighted in theirs. He experienced deep frustration and anger at not being able to work – his long spells in hospital and lengthy daily treatments at home made that impossible. And he felt frustrated, too, that he couldn't play much of an active part in the work of Mary's Meals. But towards the end of his life he found a certain peace in knowing that he could indeed do some things. He could speak to people about our work – he knew everything there was to know about it. And he could pray for it – and in doing so, he told me he even found some kind of meaning in his own daily suffering.

Like Claudio, by the end of his life Mark had discovered how to give of himself in a way that fundamentally changed him. The chronic pain, endless medical treatments and sense of isolation were things that could make him look inwards. He became trapped at times in the dark places inside himself, unable to see any light at all. Anger and self-hatred consumed him completely in his teenage years, leading him even to try to take his own life on several occasions.

Gradually, with the help of a new-found faith, he began to look outwards. A new charity was born in his heart and then a new joy when he learnt that he could indeed help other people. He did that a lot just by talking to them. A life of crippling pain and humiliation had taught him a lot. He possessed a rare wisdom about other people's suffering that allowed him to help others in pain. And his own condition, which left him weak and vulnerable, seemed to lower the barriers of other broken people so that they would open up to him about their own problems. People, myself included, would sometimes visit Mark – the sick, housebound one – partly as an act of charity, only to discover by the end of the encounter that we had been the ones receiving the charity. I often left his home more aware of my own brokenness and my need for healing – and with deep gratitude for his companionship.

By some measures Mark lived a useless life. He never completed his studies at university. He couldn't work. He never married. He was isolated from much of society. Much of what he began with relish he couldn't complete. There was so much he couldn't do. The chronic pain made it hard for him even to read much, and the painkillers he had to take meant that he couldn't drive. I have never encountered someone who experienced such prolonged, excruciating pain as Mark. In the later years of his life there were long periods when he could no longer walk. I know on many occasions he wished for it just to end. And it finally did so in a very surprising and wonderful way, in a beautiful little flower-lined field in Medjugorje. His funeral at our little village church was an amazing thing. So many people came! And as well as the raw grief there was so much joy. It turned out that the man so often housebound, with no proper hair and disfigured hands and face, had many true friendships. So many people loved him, really loved him.

Mark by the end of his life was living charity in a deep way, because he had stopped thinking about himself – even though he had a tortured body that was crying out for attention. By finding ways that he could practise charity – helping Mary's Meals in different ways and, especially, by talking to those who desperately needed to talk and be listened to – he found a new way to be. He came to possess a new peace and joy. And in doing all that, his life, like the life of little Charlie, proclaimed: 'if I can do it, so can you!'

The impact of a life devoted to charity seems to cascade down through the generations, setting off little chain reactions. In 2018, at our annual open day in the Glasgow Concert Hall, a remarkable volunteer called Bernadette Barr made this speech about her journey with Mary's Meals:

> My journey with Mary's Meals began in this very hall
> five years ago. It was my mum, Rachel's, 81st birthday
> and she chose to celebrate it here at the Mary's Meals
> day. My daughters Suzanne and Laura also came along
> and we had a really lovely day. The highlight of the day
> was the screening of the new documentary, *Child 31*. The
> hall was silent while everyone watched this powerful film
> which captured the life-changing work of MM in
> helping millions of children around the world realise
> their dreams.

It was close to the end of the film when Mum turned to me and whispered 'if only I was younger'. A simple sentiment, but one that would change my life. My mum, you see, had spent many, many years fundraising to help feed starving children. She worked tirelessly sewing, running coffee morning, fetes etc and raised tens of thousands of pounds in the process. But sadly she had been given the devastating news that she was suffering from vascular dementia and knew that her fundraising days were limited.

So, as I looked at this little lady sitting beside me and thought about her life – raising seven children with so much love and continuing to share that love with all of these poor children, I realised that I had to do whatever I could to continue her work. But what could I possibly do to follow in her amazing footsteps?

I came home and discussed it with my husband Ian and decided as cupcakes were becoming so popular that I would try my hand at baking. Not as simple as you may think as I would first have to learn how to bake! My daughter Suzanne heard of a lady holding a baking day in her home so we went along and I left with my trusty recipe in hand. My first request for cakes came from my youngest daughter Laura, a local teacher who was running a school fundraising event. And so my baking days began.

I quickly progressed to birthday cakes, christening cakes, etc and then one of my friends entrusted me with her daughter's wedding cake. I now make cakes of every size and description and with some crazy themes. I realised I needed a name for my new hobby. I chose Baked With Love, which I hope shows my love of baking but more importantly my love of knowing I am helping to feed and educate these desperately poor children. I always say my little venture is a win–win situation where I love baking and the challenge it brings, the recipient and guests enjoy the cake and for a year after their celebration children are being fed and educated.

I have moved on to running twice-yearly afternoon teas which are now so popular that the tickets are almost sold out as soon as the date is announced. I cater for 150 adults and children, where apart from an abundance of food the adults are entertained by a fabulous local musician and a wonderful group of young people from the Royal Conservatoire here in Glasgow. The children are entertained with face painting, balloon modelling and cupcake decorating etc. There is so much fun in the hall and it is great to see people catching up with friends and their generosity blows me away, with several thousand pounds being raised at each event.

Sadly, my mum passed away in October 2016. At her funeral a lady approached me saying that some 30 years ago my mum started running coffee mornings in the local church which are still running today, and they themselves have sent tens of thousands of pounds to Mary's Meals – and she insisted that had it not been for my mum's passion and living a life of example the weekly coffee mornings would not have happened.

My mum, who was such a humble and unassuming little lady, would have been so amused by the fact that the turnout at her funeral was so big that her cortège was led and followed by police motorcycles – but surely this is testimony to the love she shared with so many.

It was at this time that my husband Ian suggested sponsoring the provision of Mary's Meals at a school and naming it in memory of Mum. We have pledged to raise the £4,000 needed. To date, some 20 months later, we have actually raised approximately £23,000 for the Tombay Primary School in Liberia. Our project for the school is named Rachel's Kitchen, describing Mum's need to help feed children, and in fact her need to feed everyone who came into our family home.

The day the pictures of the school were sent to me was one of the proudest days of my life. They left both Ian and I in floods of tears. The wording on a wall of the school reads 'In memory of an astonishing woman whose vision has become a reality in Rachel's Kitchen'. Many times I think of the little children looking at those words and thinking 'who is this Rachel?' Well, she was my mum!

The audience, many of whom were moved to tears, gave a standing ovation for this woman who had created such a wonderful memorial of love for her mother. But it didn't end there. A year later Bernadette's brother, Tommy, got in touch with us. He and a friend had just cycled the length of Britain – from Land's End to John o' Groats – to raise more funds for Rachel's Kitchen. Along with his inspiring sister, he wanted to keep building that memorial to their mother and to make sure the children in Liberia kept eating. He described their adventures on the road and how along the way they would tell everyone they met about Mary's Meals. On one occasion he met a man who looked homeless – or certainly very down on his luck – and began talking to him. At first it was hard work – the man seemed sad and his answers short. Seeing their T-shirts and bicycles, he asked them what they were doing. So Tommy explained to him the work of Mary's Meals and their efforts to raise money to feed those hungry children in Liberia. The man was silent for a bit and then began to rummage in his pocket. Eventually he produced two pound coins.

'Please take it. It's all I have,' he said.

When we set off a chain reaction of giving we never know where it might end. Sometimes gifts more incredible than we could ever have imagined are given. Like the truly enormous one by the roadside that day.

Sometimes it is easier to see and understand those chains of events in hindsight. Certainly in my own life, I can now look back and understand certain things better. The story of Live Aid, which took up much of my introduction, seemed like a good way into the topic of this book as it was a relevant experience shared by many of us. But the truth is that other experiences of charity in my youth were the ones that more profoundly shaped me and led me along certain paths.

That summer of 1985 it wasn't just the smell of baking bread that pervaded our home, it was charity itself. As Mum kneaded another batch of dough, even we, despite being distracted, self-absorbed teenagers, were inclined to ask why. I can remember even then, when I learnt about what was happening, experiencing a sense of outrage that children were starving when we all had so much, and feeling a simple, unspoken conviction that such a state of affairs was unnecessary – that surely we could all do something about this. I have seen that kind of sentiment take root in the heart of many a young person since.

And my mum and dad, in time, practised much more radical acts of charity than baking bread for the local fundraising effort. Our home, a guest house from which they made their living, they eventually (at the end of story too long to tell here) gave to a Charitable Trust so it can continue to be run as the Christian retreat centre that they converted it into. Everything they accumulated from their business years has been given away to support this venture. And Mark, the brother I described above, they had initially fostered, and then formally adopted a few years before that 'summer of bread'. In doing so they provided an abandoned, emotionally disturbed boy with a new family and a new life. When parents make such radical choices in their practice of charity, the whole family become participants (whether they like it or not). Of course, as children of such a family grow towards independence they make their own choices about lifestyle and priorities – but they will have seen and experienced charity very profoundly. They will know it as a way of life that can create discomfort and even short-term angst (as the typically spoilt youngest member of a large family, I wasn't entirely happy at the prospect of losing that status to a disturbed, angry little stranger from the city). But they will also know that ultimately such a life provides meaning and creates joy. And that short-term angst inevitably becomes a blessing (in my own life, that annoying little boy who suddenly intruded on my cosy family situation became another very dear brother and a profound blessing in all our lives).

Samuel, the son of Karel and Lucy in the Czech Republic, will not yet understand the choice his parents made to give up their dream home for Mary's Meals. I have no idea how he will feel about it when he does. But I do have a conviction that his life will be much more profoundly blessed by that choice than any kind of physical house they might have chosen to build – or any other material benefit for that matter.

Our kids don't grow up happier because at some point we managed to buy a nicer family car – even if we kid ourselves that they will. They don't become more joyful adults because they grew up in a house with two spare bedrooms rather than having to share theirs with a sibling or two. And they won't be adults with a stronger sense of identity and a deeper sense of who they really are because their parents could afford to buy them clothes with fashionable brand names on them. 'For where our treasure is, our heart will be also': We do not need to know our Scripture or be a Christian to know the truth of that statement.

To be denied such material things by acts of charity might be the biggest blessing our parents could ever bestow upon us. Parents who love that much are the best of parents. They are the ones providing the most precious inheritances to their children and their children afterwards. For that kind of treasure is not being depleted by each generation, like an exhaustible seam of coal. The question of sustainability does not apply to love itself – although love might well lead us to ask questions about sustainable development and the care of creation, because love, of course, desires a good life for our children.

But parents don't need to make radical, life-changing deci-sions to be wonderful parents – or to impart charity. In fact, none of us do whether we are parents or not. The great figures of history who defeated injustice, the wonderful saints of old who kissed lepers and sold themselves into slavery, the remarkable women who have taken vows to spend every day of their life performing works of charity, show us what charity can look like; how very beautiful it can be. But most of us aren't called to that. Instead we are only called to say some-thing nice to the difficult child in the playground who the rest of our school mates don't want to talk to, or to visit the family in our street newly arrived from a faraway place, or to drive our sick, housebound neighbour to the hospital. The women of my village who head to the kitchen of our village hall every time there is a local funeral with their homemade soup and sandwiches, as a gift to the grieving family and friends who gather there after the graveside prayers – they are practising charity of that sort, not for any rewards, or accolades, or future success to work towards. There is nothing here that looks as if it is going to transform our world. This sort of charity is pure, unpolluted by ambition and unspoilt by us charity workers, who in our eagerness to lead charity and tell other people how to do it, sometimes tarnish the precious thing that first stole our hearts.

When I see people like those makers of the soup and sandwiches, I think of Mary the mother of Jesus. Despite being the most famous woman who ever lived, and certainly the most loved and revered, she never seemed to do anything eye-catching or dramatic in her own right. In fact Scripture records only a very few words spoken by her. The only lengthy passage of speech is the Magnificat, when she quotes the Old Testament to praise God as the one 'who has filled the starving with good things, sent the rich empty away' (Luke 1:53, NJB). Here she speaks for the poor and gives voice to her rich faith and trust in a God of mercy. She spoke this famous hymn of praise when she went to meet her cousin Elizabeth, who was also pregnant, to be with her and help her. To get there Mary travelled about a hundred miles, probably by donkey. Mary was a woman of quiet practical charity, and incredibly brave charity too – so brave it led her to remain at the cross, deliberately in sight, as her son died an awful death.

When we think of the analogy of the stars that guide us in the night on our journey towards dawn, we might also remember the moon, that lights our way with a very special gentle light. We might think of Mary as the moon in that imagery. Because, while she is not the source of the light, she reflects it in a wonderful way. By its light the moon tells us that the sun is still there shining, and that it is only hidden for a little while. It helps us wait patiently for dawn. And many a traveller on an otherwise dark night has the moon to thank for finding their way home.

Each of us can choose to go on with the little quiet things, pouring all the love we can find in our hearts into them, even if it feels like we haven't found very much. We may discover as we go on that our hearts are growing little by little, and that in them our love grows too.

And we do not need to wait until we feel good about ourselves in order to begin. If we find ourselves trapped in a shadow dark as death, bound by self-pity or self-hate with no way out, then let us begin anyway. We have nothing to lose by lighting one little candle for our neighbour. We do not have to believe we are good in order to do something good, but when we try it (doing something good) we may find that, in fact, there is indeed something good in us after all. We don't need to feel complete, or in control, or impressive in any way to light that candle. And when we do that for our neighbour the light will shine a little on us too. More of our very selves will be revealed to us and we will see that the darkness lied to us and that we really aren't that ugly after all. And the darkness, having been found out, will take flight, in fear of the rising sun, in fear of that newly discovered thing growing in our hearts.

Epilogue

Towards the end of a midwinter afternoon I went for a walk with my seven-year-old son, Gabriel. The snow down in our glen had melted disappointingly quickly and both of us felt drawn to the deep white drifts high on the hill behind our house. As we climbed up a path that I have walked with my own father a thousand times, we spooked a herd of hungry deer on their way down looking for night-time grass in the lower fields. Even though we hadn't planned to go so far, we soon found ourselves on top of the hill, 1,000 feet above our house, which we could just about make out amid the trees – or at least the smoke drifting from its chimney. The lights of our village were now twinkling along the river, above which a mist was starting to rise. Gabriel managed to spot his school on the other side, and the village hall and then the train station – in fact a train, too, chugging out towards Oban, crossing the bridge where the river flowed into Loch Awe. Above it the dramatic peaks of Cruachan, which towered much higher than our hill, were catching some big black clouds as they rolled in towards us from the Atlantic.

'We'd better get going before it gets dark,' I said.

The temperature was plummeting and the snow was freezing hard again now. Almost immediately on starting our journey down we both lost our footing and fell, laughing into the snow. I held Gabriel's hand as we approached a steeper part of the path.

'Let's just be careful on this bit,' I cautioned.

But it was me who slipped next. My standing foot slithered on the ice and, as I began to lose my balance, I tried to let go of Gabriel's hand so that I didn't pull him over. But he held surprisingly firm and I just managed to stay on my feet.

We both laughed.

'If anyone was watching us now, they would think it was me helping you down the hill, but I am not so sure!' I said.

'Well, Dad, it is just that we are both helping each other,' Gabriel said as if to reassure me.

And almost immediately I slithered once more and again a strong little hand kept me from falling.

'But I am helping you a lot more that you are helping me!' he gurgled through an explosion of laughter.

Acknowledgements

Thank you Julie, once again, for your abundant encouragement in the writing of this book. Thank you for putting up so patiently with the 'author version' of your husband – one who is even more distracted and insecure than usual. And thanks to all of my children for helping in different ways – Calum and Ben, thanks for reading the manuscript and making encouraging noises; Martha, Toby and Bethany, thanks for patiently sharing our dodgy Wi-Fi even when you had homework to do; and Anna and Gabriel, thanks for letting me have part of our dining room table when you had pictures to draw and your own stories to write.

A huge thanks also to all my co-workers in the Mary's Meals movement for teaching me, a slow learner, about charity. Thank you for your innumerable acts of love – both the mundane and the extraordinary. Every day you humble me and inspire me. I hope this book does justice to what you have taught me.

I would also like to give special thanks to those who have provided precious advice, especially Maria Byars, Charles McGhee, Leah Swindon, Bishop John Keenan and Sonia Land.

I would also like to thank all those at HarperCollins who have patiently guided me on this project – Carlos Darby especially.

And to You, my God, be all praise and thanksgiving. Thank you for loving us first.